1000 FACTS ON

BIRDS

First published in 2002 by Miles Kelly Publishing Ltd
Bardfield Centre, Great Bardfield
Essex, CM7 4SL

Some material in this book first appeared in *1000 Things You Should Know About Birds*

2 4 6 8 10 9 7 5 3 1

Editors
Ruth Boardman, Nicola Jessop, Isla MacCuish

Design
Venita Kidwai

Index
Jane Parker

Picture Research
Liberty Newton

British Library Cataloguing-in-Publication Data
A catalogue record for this book is available from the British Library

ISBN 1-84236-149-X
Printed in Hong Kong

www.mileskelly.net
info@mileskelly.net

1000 FACTS ON

BIRDS

Jinny Johnson
Consultant Steve Parker

MiLeS
KeLLy
PUBLISHING

Contents

How birds live
The world of birds 8; Early birds 10; The structure of birds 12; Beaks and feet 14; Feathers 16; Nests 18; Eggs 20; Caring for young 22; Bird song and calls 24; Bird senses 26; Migration 28; Endangered birds 30; Desert birds 32; Rainforest birds 34; Grassland birds 36; Polar and tundra birds 38

4

Perching birds

Crows 40; Swallows and martins 42; Larks and wagtails 44; Weavers and relatives 46; Fairy-wrens and relatives 48; Parrots 50; Warblers 52; Manakins and Cotingas 54; Tyrant flycatchers 56; Old World flycatchers 58; Vireos and relatives 60; Nuthatches and relatives 62; Mockingbirds and relatives 64; Shrikes and vangas 66; Pittas and relatives 68; Buntings and tanagers 70; Bowerbirds 72; Antbirds and tapaculos 74; Finches and relatives 76; Thrushes and dippers 78; Wrens and babblers 80; Sunbirds and relatives 82; Lyrebirds and relatives 84; Ovenbirds and relatives 86; Old World sparrows 88; Drongos and relatives 90; Waxwings and relatives 92; Wood warblers and icterids 94; Bulbuls and relatives 96; Tits 98; Birds of paradise 100; Starlings 102; Monarchs and relatives 104

Contents

Owls and birds of prey
Hawks and harriers 106; Falcons 108; Buzzards, kites and osprey 110; Owls 112; Snake and sea eagles 114; True and harpy eagles 116; New World vultures 118; Old World vultures 120

Water and wading birds
Avocets and relatives 122; Plovers and lapwings 124; Pelicans 126; Storks 128; Cranes and trumpeters 130; Ibises and relatives 132; Herons and bitterns 134; Rails and bustards 136; Finfoots and relatives 138; Ducks 140; Geese and swans 142; Sandpipers 144; Terns and skimmers 146; Gulls and relatives 148; Shearwaters and petrels 150; Oystercatchers and relatives 152; Auks 154; Large seabirds 156; Penguins 158; Divers and grebes 160; Cormorants and anhingas 162; Gannets and boobies 164

Contents

Game and ground birds
Mesites and relatives 166;
Ostriches and emu 168;
Partridges and relatives 170;
Pheasants and relatives 172;
Turkeys and grouse 174;
Megapodes and guans 176;
Cassowaries and kiwis 178;
Rheas and tinamous 180

Woodland and forest birds
Toucans and honeyguides 182;
Hornbills 184; Woodpeckers
186; Bee-eaters and relatives
188; Swifts 190; Cuckoos and
hoatzin 192; Kingfishers 194;
Nightjars and relatives
196; Jacamars and
relatives 198;
Pigeons and
sandgrouse 200;
Hummingbirds
202; Hoopoes
and relatives 204;
Mousebirds and
trogons 206

The world of birds

- **There are more than 9000 species** of birds.

- **One of the most widespread** of all birds is the osprey, which is found nearly all over the world.

- **More than a third of all known bird species** live and breed in South and Central America.

- **A species** is a particular type of bird. Birds of the same species can mate and have young, and these can themselves have offspring.

- **The 9000 bird species** are organized into about 180 families. Species in a family share certain characteristics such as body shape.

- **Bird families** are organized into 28 or 29 larger groups called orders. Largest is the perching bird order, with more than 5000 bird species.

- **The wandering albatross** is one of the longest-lived birds. Individuals may live as long as 50 years.

- **The red-billed quelea** is probably the most common wild bird. There are thought to be at least 1.5 billion.

▲ *Ospreys make a large nest in a tree or on a cliff. They feed mostly on fish, which they snatch from the water with their feet.*

- **The largest bird,** the ostrich, weighs almost 80,000 times more than the smallest, the bee hummingbird.

- **All birds** lay hard-shelled eggs, in which their young develop. If a mother bird had young that developed inside her body instead, she would be too heavy to fly.

◄ *Many birds are highly sociable, flocking together to feed and raise their young.*

9

Early birds

- **The earliest known bird** is *Archaeopteryx*, which lived 155–150 million years ago. It had feathers like a modern bird but teeth like a reptile.

- **Ichthyornis** was a seabird with long, toothed jaws. It lived alongside dinosaurs in the Late Cretaceous period.

- **Although it could fly**, *Archaeopteryx* could not take off from the ground, and probably had to climb a tree before launching itself into the air.

- **Scientists believe** that birds evolved from lightly built dinosaurs such as *Compsognathus*, which ran on two legs.

- **The dodo** stood 1 m tall and lived on the island of Mauritius. It became extinct in the 17th century.

◀ Archaeopteryx *had a wingspan of about 50 cm. Its name means 'ancient wing'.*

10

- *Aepyornis* (also known as the 'elephant bird'), a 3-m tall ostrich ancestor from Madagascar, probably became extinct in the 17th century.

- **The eggs** of *Aepyornis* may have weighed as much as 10 kg – more than 9 times the weight of an ostrich egg today.

- **The tallest bird ever** was the moa (*Dinornis*) of New Zealand. It was a towering 3.5 m tall.

- **The great auk** first lived 2 million years ago. It became extinct in the mid 19th century after being overhunted for its fat, which was burned in oil lamps.

- **An early member** of the vulture family, *Argentavix* of South America had an amazing 7.3 m wingspan.

▶ *Like today's seabirds,* Ichthyornis *probably fed on fish which it caught in its long toothed jaws.*

11

The structure of birds

- **Birds are the only creatures** to have feathers. These keep them warm and protected from the weather and allow them to fly.

- **Like mammals, fish and reptiles**, a bird is a vertebrate animal – this means that it has a backbone.

- **Birds** have a body temperature of 40°C to 44°C – higher than other warm-blooded animals.

- **A bird's bones** have a honeycomb structure. The bones are so light that they account for only about 5% of its total weight.

- **Birds** do not have teeth. Instead their food is ground down by a part of the digestive system called the gizzard. Some birds swallow small stones to help the action of the gizzard.

- **A bird's nostrils** are usually at the base of the beak, but in the kiwi, which has a better sense of smell than most birds, they are at the tip.

- **Birds' muscles** make up 30–60% of their total weight. The biggest are the flight and leg muscles.

- **Small birds** have about 15 neck vertebrae, while the mute swan has 23. (Mammals have only 7.)

◀ *Thrushes are adaptable birds, able to feed on fruit as well as insects.*

- **The skeleton** of a bird's wings has a similar structure to the human arm, but the wrist bones are joined. Also, a bird has much reduced bones for three fingers, not five fingers like us.

- **The heart rate** of a tiny hummingbird reaches an astonishing 615 beats a minute when in mid-flight.

A bird's external nostrils are usually near the base of the upper beak

Some of a bird's bones are not solid and have a honeycombed structure. These are strong but light, allowing the bird to fly.

A bird's heart is large for its body size.

Beaks and feet

- **No bird** has more than four toes, but some have three and the ostrich has only two.

- **Four-toed birds** have different arrangements of toes: in swifts, all four point forwards; in most perching birds, three point forwards and one backwards; and in parrots, two point forwards and two backwards.

- **A beak** is made up of a bird's projecting jaw bones, covered in a hard horny material.

- **The hyacinth macaw** has one of the most powerful beaks of any bird, strong enough to crack brazil nuts.

- **Webbed feet** make all waterbirds very efficient paddlers.

- **The Australian pelican** has the largest beak of any bird, at up to 50 cm long.

- **Nightjars** have the shortest beaks, at 8–10 mm long.

◀ *The sword-billed hummingbird has an extremely long beak and a long tongue for extracting nectar from flowers.*

▶ *The crossbill is so-called because the upper and lower portions of its beak cross over one another.*

▼ *Below is the foot of a bird of prey. Its long, curving talons make deadly weapons.*

. . . FASCINATING FACT . . .
A baby bird has a spike called an 'egg-tooth' on its beak for breaking its way out of its egg.

● **A bird stands** on the tips of its toes – the backward bending joint halfway down its leg is the ankle joint.

● **A bird's beak** is extremely sensitive to touch. Birds that probe in the ground for food have extra sensory organs at the beak tip.

15

Feathers

- **Feathers** are made of a protein called keratin. Human hair and nails are also made of keratin.

- **Feathers grow** at a rate of 1–13 mm a day.

- **The ruby-throated hummingbird** has only 940 feathers, while the whistling swan has 25,216.

- **A bird's feathers** are replaced once or twice a year in a process that is known as 'moulting'.

- **Feathers** keep a bird warm, protect its skin, provide a flight surface, and may also attract mates.

- **In most birds**, a third of the feathers are on the head.

- **The longest feathers ever known** were 10.59 m long, and belonged to an ornamental chicken.

- **The feathers** that cover a bird's body are called contour feathers. Down feathers underneath provide extra warmth.

- **The 7182 feathers** of a bald eagle weighed 677 g, more than twice as much as the bird's skeleton.

- **Birds** spend time every day 'preening' – cleaning and rearranging their feathers with their beaks.

▶ *The peacock has the most ornate feathers of any bird.*

Nests

- **The bald eagle** makes the biggest nest of any bird. It can be as large as 2.5 m across and 3.5 m deep – big enough for several people to hide inside!

- **The bee hummingbird's nest** is the smallest – only the size of a thimble.

- **The hammerkop**, a heron-like bird, makes a huge nest up to 2 m high and weighing 50 kg.

- **The hammerkop uses anything** from sticks to bits of bone and plastic to make its nest.

- **A cliff swallow's nest** is made up of about 1200 tiny balls of mud.

- **Nightjars** do not make a nest – they just lay their eggs on the ground.

- **Hummingbirds** and honeyeaters use spiders' webs to hold their nests together.

◀ *Between them, birds can nest almost anywhere, in holes, tree trunks, even on the sides of cliffs!*

- **The rufous-breasted castle builde**r (woodcreeper family) makes a nest shaped like a dumb-bell. It has two chambers – one for the chicks.

- **The turquoise-browed motmot** is a surprisingly efficient digger, excavating a 1.5-m long burrow in just 5 days.

- **The European bee-eater** nests underground to keep cool. While the surface temperature may reach 50°C, the bee-eater's nest remains a pleasant 25°C.

▼ *A bald eagle's nest is used and enlarged year after year.*

Eggs

- **All bird species** lay eggs.

- **The biggest egg** is the ostrich egg. At 1.5 kg, it is 30 times heavier than an average hen's egg.

- **Incubation** is the process of keeping eggs warm while they develop. It can take from 10–80 days.

- **The yellow yolk** in an egg provides food for the growing embryo. The white provides food and moisture.

- **Gannets stand on their eggs** to keep them warm!

- **Egg yolks** are not always yellow. The common tern's yolk is deep red, and the gentoo penguin's a pinky red.

First tiny hole

Egg cracks

Chick appears

▲ *When a chick is ready to hatch, it makes a tiny hole in the shell with its 'egg-tooth' – a process called 'pipping' – and then struggles out.*

Chick breaks free of egg

> ...FASCINATING FACT...
> The bee hummingbird lays the smallest egg at
> 0.3 g. You could fit 4700 into one ostrich egg!

- **The shell of an egg** contains 50–100 tiny pores per sq cm. This means that oxygen can pass through the shell to the baby bird inside and carbon dioxide can pass out.

- **Eggshells** vary in thickness from 0.2 mm in the night heron's egg to 0.75 mm in the common murre's.

- **Not all eggs are oval** – those of owls and toucans are round, and auks lay pear-shaped eggs.

◄ A bird's egg,
though seemingly
simple, contains
everything that
the growing
embryo inside
needs to survive.

21

Caring for young

- **Many baby birds** are blind, naked and helpless when they hatch, and have to be cared for by their parents.

- **The young of ducks and geese** hatch with a covering of feathers, and can find food hours after hatching.

- **A young golden eagle** has grown feathers after 50 days and learned to fly after 70, but stays with its parents for another month while learning to hunt.

- **A young bird** is known as a fledgling from the time it hatches until it is fully feathered and can fly.

- **A young pelican** feeds by putting its head deep into its parent's large beak and gobbling up any fish it finds.

- **A swan** carries its young on its back to keep them safe.

- **To obtain food** from its parent, a young herring gull has to peck at a red spot on the parent's beak. The adult gull then regurgitates food for the chick to eat.

▶ *Swans are attentive parents – the female usually incubates the eggs but but the male is equally involved in raising the young. Chicks are tended for about five months after they hatch.*

- **Shearwaters** feed their young for 60 days, then stop. After a week the chicks get so hungry that they take to the air to find food for themselves.

- **In 3 weeks,** a new-born cuckoo gets 50 times heavier.

> **FASCINATING FACT**
> In a colony of thousands of birds, baby terns can recognize the call of their own parents.

▼ *Bokmakierie shrike chicks are born blind, but their eyes are open by four days old.*

23

Bird song and calls

- **Birds** make two sorts of sounds – simple calls, giving a warning or a threat, and the more complicated songs sung by some males at breeding time.

- **Birds' songs** have a definite dialect. The songs of a group of chaffinches in one area, will sound slightly different from those of a group somewhere else.

- **A songbird** reared in captivity away from its family produces a weak version of its parents' song, but cannot perform the whole repertoire.

- **Gulls and parrots** do not sing, but they do make various calls to attract mates or warn off enemies.

- **A bird sings** by vibrating the thin muscles in its syrinx – a special organ in its throat.

- **A sedge warbler** may use at least 50 different sounds in its songs.

▶ *The chaffinch is the commonest of Europe's finches and has a cheerful, attractive song.*

◀ *Skylarks make special, fluttering flights accompanied by a distinctive song.*

- **Male and female boubou shrikes** sing a duet together, performing alternate parts of the song.

- **Songbirds** may make as many as 20 calls; gulls make only about 10.

- **Birds** make other sounds, too. During courtship flights, male woodpigeons make a loud clapping with their wings.

... FASCINATING FACT ...
A baby songbird starts to learn to sing about 10 days after it hatches, and continues to learn for about 40 days.

Bird senses

- **Almost all birds** have excellent sight, and most depend on their eyes for finding food.

- **A bird's outer ear** consists of a short tube leading from the eardrum to the outside. In most birds the ear openings are just behind the jaw.

- **A barn owl's hearing** is so good that it can detect and catch prey in complete darkness without using its eyes at all.

- **A chicken** has only 24 tastebuds and a starling about 200 – a human has 9000.

- **An eagle** can spot prey from as much as 1.6 km above the Earth.

- **A starling's eye** is as much as 15% of the total weight of its head. A human's eye is only 1% of the head weight.

- **An ostrich's eye**, at 5 cm in diameter, is larger than any other land animal's eye.

◄ *Using its amazing hearing, the barn owl can hunt mice and other small rodents at night.*

▶ *Birds of prey, like this eagle, swoop down on their victims, using their powerful, crushing talons more than their beak to make the kill.*

- **Birds** are 10 times more sensitive to changes of pitch and intensity in sounds than humans. They can detect sounds of 1/200 second.

- **Kiwis have poor sight** and depend more on their sense of smell for finding many food items, such as earthworms, at night.

- **Albatrosses** have a good sense of smell. In experiments, they have been attracted to food from a distance of 30 km.

27

Migration

- **Migration** is the journey made twice a year between a summer breeding area, where food is plentiful, and a wintering area with a good climate.

- **Many migrating birds** have to build up fat stores to allow them to fly non-stop for many days without food.

- **A migrating bird** can fly across the Sahara Desert in 50–60 hours without stopping to 'refuel'.

- **Birds find their way** by observing landmarks, the patterns of stars and the position of the setting sun. They also use their sense of smell and monitor the Earth's magnetic field.

- **Most birds** that migrate long distances fly at night.

- **The snow goose** migrates nearly 5000 km south from Arctic Canada at an altitude of 9000 m.

- **Before migration was studied**, some people thought swallows simply spent the winter asleep in mud.

- **Even flightless birds migrate**. Emus make journeys on foot of 500 km or more, and penguins migrate in water.

- **Every year** at least 5 billion birds migrate from North to Central and South America.

- **The Arctic tern** spends the northern summer in the Arctic and migrates to the Antarctic for the southern summer, enjoying 24 hours of daylight in both places.

▶ *Geese migrate in huge flocks, but pairs stay together within the flock.*

Endangered birds

- **More than 80 species of parrot**, such as the hyacinth macaw, are in danger of extinction or are very rare.

- **At least 1000 bird species** now face extinction – 30 or so became extinct in the 1900s.

- **The Hawaiian mamo** (Hawaiian honeycreeper family) became extinct in 1899, partly because more than 80,000 birds were killed to make a cloak for King Kamehameha I.

- **There are only about 600** black-faced spoonbills left.

◀ *The hyacinth macaw has suffered from illegal hunting for the pet trade and from habitat destruction. It is now bred in captivity.*

↖ Once in danger of extinction, the American bald eagle population has now recovered, thanks to a captive breeding programme.

> ...FASCINATING FACT...
> The bald eagle was threatened by the harmful effects of DDT on its eggs, but has recovered since the pesticide was banned in 1972.

- **The Fiji petrel** was first discovered on the island of Gau Fiji in 1855, and was not seen again until 1984. Numbers are thought to be low.

- **Probably less than 1000** red siskins remain in the wild – it has been a popular cage-bird since the mid 1800s.

- **The Floreana mockingbird** disappeared from one of the Galapagos Islands because rats were introduced.

- **The short-tailed albatross** has long been exploited for its feathers, and has been extremely rare since 1930.

- **In New Zealand**, Hutton's shearwater is preyed on by introduced stoats, while deer trample its burrows.

Desert birds

- **The little cinnamon quail-thrush** of Australia hides in a burrow during the day to escape the hot sun and comes out in the evening to find seeds and insects to eat.

- **The verdin** lives in the deserts of Mexico and the southwest of the USA, where it makes its nest on a cactus plant. The cactus spines protect the verdin and its eggs from predators.

- **With few trees and bushes to sit in**, desert birds spend most of their lives on the ground.

- **The mourning dove** is a desert bird of the southwestern USA. A fast flier, it often travels great distances to find food and water.

- **Turkey vultures** soar over the American desert searching for carrion to eat.

▶ *Sandgrouse are suited to extreme desert conditions, withstanding soaring temperatures with little need for water. They are also strong fliers and travel long distances to find water.*

- **Insects** are a favourite food of many desert birds, but some catch small mammals and others eat seeds.
- **Most desert birds** are active at dawn and towards sunset, resting in shade for much of the day.
- **Owls, poorwills and nightjars** cool down in the desert heat by opening their mouths wide and fluttering their throats.
- **Water is precious in the desert.** The roadrunner, a member of the cuckoo family, reabsorbs water from its faeces before excreting them.

▲ *The greater roadrunner lives in the western USA, where it preys on small snakes as well as insects and mice.*

· · · FASCINATING FACT · · ·
Desert-living bird species are usually smaller than those found elsewhere in the world.

33

Rainforest birds

- **Male and female eclectus parrots** of the Amazon rainforest have very different plumage. The male bird is mostly bright green, while the female is red with a blue underside.

- **The crowned eagle** lives in African rainforests, where it feeds on monkeys and other mammals such as mongooses and rats.

- **The king vulture** of South America is the only vulture to live in rainforest. As well as feeding on carrion, it also kills mammals and reptiles.

- **The sunbittern** lives along river banks in the rainforests of South America, feeding on frogs, insects and other creatures.

- **With its abundance** of flowers, leaves, fruits and insects all year round, a rainforest is the ideal home for many different kinds of birds.

- **The muscovy duck** is now familiar in farmyards and parks in many parts of the world. However, it originally came from the rainforests of Central and South America.

- **Large, flightless cassowaries** live in the rainforests of New Guinea, where people hunt them to eat.

- **The spectacled eagle owl** of South America has rings of white feathers around its eyes. Its call resembles the hammering sound made by woodpeckers.

- **The rare Cassin's hawk eagle** lives in African rainforests, and hunts squirrels and other birds.

> **FASCINATING FACT**
> The hoatzin builds its nest over rainforest rivers, so that if its chicks are threatened, they can drop into the water to escape.

Huge eagles nest at the tops of the highest rainforest trees

▼ *The tropical rainforest has more types of bird than anywhere else. Many of the birds in the canopy are amazingly colourful. Game birds and little insect eaters patrol the forest floor.*

The stunning, resplendent quetzal favours trees of the laurel family

Macaws, parrots, toucans and many other species flutter through the rainforest canopy

Grassland birds

- **The yellow-billed oxpecker** of the African grasslands sits on buffaloes' backs, pulling ticks from their skin.

- **Flocks of 1 million or more** red-billed quelea are seen moving like vast clouds over southern Africa.

- **The grasslands of South America** are home to the red-legged seriema, a long-legged, fast-running bird that eats virtually anything it can find, including snakes.

▲ *Secretary birds are so-called because of the quill-like crests on the backs of their heads.*

- **Unlike most hornbills**, the southern ground hornbill of southern Africa spends most of its time on the ground.

- **One of the biggest creatures** on the South American pampas is the rhea, which feeds mainly on grass.

- **Cattle egrets** accompany large grassland mammals, feeding on the insects that live on or around them.

> ... **FASCINATING FACT** ...
> A fast walker, the long-legged secretary bird of the African grasslands may travel 30 km a day in search of snakes, insects and birds.

- **The crested oropendola** is a grassland bird of South America. It hunts insects and other small creatures.

- **North America's largest owl**, the great horned owl, includes other grassland birds such as quail in its diet.

- **The western meadowlark** makes a ground nest of grass and pine needles in prairie grasslands.

▼ *The red-billed quelea is a common sight in grassland areas across the southern African continent.*

▲ *The oxpecker is so-called because it often pecks at wounds in the skin of grassland mammals, like buffalo, whilst pulling ticks from their skin.*

37

Polar and tundra birds

- **The willow ptarmigan** lives on the Arctic tundra. In winter it has white feathers that help to keep it hidden in the snow, but in summer it grows darker feathers again.

- **The ivory gull** of Arctic coasts and islands is the only all-white gull.

- **Adélie penguins** breed on coasts and islands around the Antarctic in huge colonies that return to the same site year after year.

- **Snowy owls** are among the fiercest Arctic birds. They soar over the tundra preying on other birds and small mammals such as lemmings.

▶ *The snowy owl's white feathers help to camouflage it in its Arctic home.*

- **Most birds leave Antarctica in winter,** but the southern black-backed gull stays all year round. It feeds on fish and birds' eggs as well as some carrion.

- **The emperor penguin** breeds in colder temperatures than any other bird. It can survive temperatures of -40°C as it incubates its egg.

- **The great skua** is the biggest flying bird in Antarctica, at up to 5 kg and 66 cm long.

- **Although only 10 cm long,** the little storm petrel may migrate 40,000 km a year between the two poles.

- **The laysan albatross** breeds on central Pacific islands, but spends most of the year flying over the Arctic hunting for schools of fish to eat.

- **Tufted puffins** nest only on cliffs and islands in the Arctic North Pacific. One colony contained as many as one million nests.

▲ *In winter, the willow grouse feeds mainly on the twigs and buds of dwarf willows and other trees.*

39

Crows

- **Members of the crow family** live on all continents of the world, except Antarctica. There are about 117 species, including jackdaws, rooks, ravens, nutcrackers, choughs and jays, as well as common crows.

- **Bold and aggressive**, a typical crow is a big bird with a strong body and legs, and a powerful beak that can deal with nuts, seeds and even small prey.

- **At 66 cm long**, the raven is the largest of the crow family, and the largest of the songbird group of birds.

- **Crows** are thought to be among the most intelligent of all birds. Studies on ravens have shown that they are able to count up to five or six.

- **When food is plentiful**, nutcrackers hide nuts and pine seeds in holes in the ground, and are able to find them again months later.

> **FASCINATING FACT**
> Magpies steal the eggs and young of other birds, as well as bright, shiny objects such as jewellery, which they hide in their nests.

- **There are many superstitions** about ravens – the arrival of a raven is said to be an evil omen and a sign of an imminent death.

- **A species of crow** that lives on the Pacific island of New Caledonia uses tools such as hooked twigs and sharp-ended stems to extract grubs from the crowns of palm trees.

- **Breeding pairs** of Australian white-winged choughs use a team of up to eight other choughs to help them find food for their young.

- **Some crows in Japan** have learned how to get cars to crack nuts for them. They put the nuts in front of cars at traffic lights, wait for the cars to pass over them, and collect the kernels once the lights are red again!

▼ *The secret of the crow's success is its adaptability. Crows eat a wide range of foods and are intelligent enough to learn how to make use of new food sources. Shown here are: (1) the raven, (2) the rook, (3) the hooded crow, (4) the chough, (5) the jackdaw.*

41

Swallows and martins

- **There are about 80 species of swallows and martins** found all over the world. Most migrate between breeding grounds and wintering areas.

- **The sand martin** digs a 120 cm long nesting burrow in riverbanks.

- **Only discovered in 1968,** the white-eyed river martin spends the winter in reedbeds on Lake Boraphet in Thailand.

- **Purple martins** often nest in old woodpecker holes or in nest-boxes. The female incubates the 4–5 eggs alone, but the male helps feed the young.

- **There is an old saying** that the weather will be good when swallows fly high, but bad when swallows fly low. This is based on fact – in wet weather, insects stay nearer the ground, so their predators – the swallows – do the same.

- **Adult swallows** will carry a mass of crushed insects, squashed in a ball in the throat, back to their young. A barn swallow may take 400 meals a day to its chicks.

◀ *The house martin often lives near people, making its nest under the eaves of buildings or under bridges or other structures.*

- **Sand martins** breed in the northern hemisphere, migrating south in the winter in flocks of thousands.

- **In most swallow species,** males and females are alike, but in the rare blue swallow, the female has a short tail, while the male's is long and forked.

- **Swallows** catch their insect food in the air as they fly.

▲ *Swallows may lay up to eight eggs at a time, often in 'mud cups' attached to buildings.*

> ...FASCINATING FACT...
> The ancient Romans used swallows as messengers to carry news of the winners of chariot races to neighbouring towns.

Larks and wagtails

- **The shore lark** has the widest distribution of any lark. Its habitats range from the icy Arctic to deserts.

- **The wagtail family** has about 60 species, most of which are small, insect-eating birds. They include pipits and longclaws.

- **The 75 species of lark** live in North America, parts of South America, Africa, Europe, Asia and Australia. The greatest number of species is found in Africa.

FASCINATING FACT
The yellow-throated longclaw gets its name from the 5-cm long claw on each back toe.

▲ Also called the horned lark, the shore lark is found in the far north of Europe as well as in North America, North Africa and Asia.

- **The female skylark** makes a shallow, grassy nest on the ground, and incubates 3–4 eggs.

- **The skylark** performs a beautiful song as it flutters up to a great height, hovers and descends again.

- **The thick-billed lark** has a larger, stronger beak than most larks, and uses it to crush hard seeds and tough-shelled insects.

- **The shore or horned lark** is the only member of the family to live in the Americas.

- **The desert lark's** colouration varies according to where it lives – birds in areas of white sand have pale feathers, while those that live on dark laval sand are almost black.

- **Craneflies** are one of the favourite foods of the meadow pipit. Adults may feed their 3–5 chicks on craneflies for 2 weeks. The chicks develop in a nest of dry grass lined with down.

▶ *The little pied wagtail bobs its tail up and down almost all the time as it searches for insects.*

45

Weavers and relatives

◀ *When the male cape weaver has finished making a nest, it calls to the female.*

● **The sociable weaver** nests in groups of up to 300 birds. The huge nest is made of sticks and grass, normally in a large acacia tree. It may measure 4 m deep and weigh up to 1000 kg. Each pair of birds has its own hole in the nest.

● **Desert-living sociable weavers** use their nest all year round for shelter from sun, wind and cold. At night, when temperatures drop, the nest holes stay 20°C warmer than the outside air.

● **Whydah birds** do not make their own nests, but lay their eggs in the nests of other birds, usually waxbills.

● **Young whydahs** make the same sounds and have the same mouth markings as their foster parents' own young, and because of this they get fed.

> ····· FASCINATING FACT ·····
> As many as 500 pairs of
> red-billed queleas may nest
> together in one acacia tree.

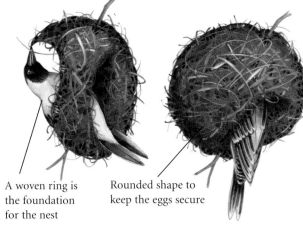

A woven ring is the foundation for the nest

Rounded shape to keep the eggs secure

▲ *The male weaver bird generally makes the nest, using his beak and feet to weave and knot material together.*

Long entrance tunnel makes it difficult for any predators to enter the nest

- **The baya weaver** makes a beautiful nest of woven grass and leaves that it hangs from a tree or roof.

- **In the breeding season**, the male paradise whydah grows 28 cm long tail feathers – almost twice the length of its body – for display in flight.

- **Most weavers** have short, strong beaks that they use for feeding on seeds and insects.

- **The red bishop** mates with three or four females, who all nest in his territory.

- **The red-vented malimbe** (a weaver) feeds mainly on the husks of oil palm nuts.

Fairy-wrens and relatives

- **The 26 species of fairy-wrens** live in Australia and New Guinea, where they forage for insects on the ground.

- **Young fairy-wrens** often stay with their parents and help them raise the next brood of young. Pairs with helpers can raise more young than those without.

- **The rock warbler** makes its nest in a dark cave or mine-shaft, attaching the nest to the walls with spider webs.

- **During its courtship display**, the male superb fairy-wren may present his mate with a yellow flower petal.

- **If a predator** comes too close to a fairy-wren's nest, the parent birds make a special 'rodent run' away from the nest, squeaking and trailing their tails to confuse and distract the enemy.

◀ *The male superb fairy-wren is easily recognized by the bright blue plumage around his head and neck.*

- **The 50 or so species of thickhead** live in rainforests and scrub in Southeast Asia and Australasia.

- **The white-throated gerygone's nest** hangs from a eucalyptus branch and is made from bark strips and plant fibres woven together with spider webs.

- **The hooded pitohui** (thickhead family) is one of the very few poisonous birds known. Its feathers and skin contain a poison that protects it from predators.

- **The Australasian warbler** family includes 65 species of gerygone, thornbills and scrubwrens.

- **The golden whistler** is probably the most variable of birds – the 70 or more races all have slightly different feather patterns or beak shapes.

◀ The white-throated gerygone belongs to the Australasian warbler family, found in Australia, New Zealand and adjacent islands.

49

Parrots

- **The only flightless parrot** is the New Zealand kakapo or owl parrot, which is now extremely rare.

- **The palm cockatoo** has an amazing courtship display. The male bird holds a stick in its foot and makes a loud drumming noise by beating the stick against the side of a tree.

- **At about 85 cm long**, the scarlet macaw of South and Central America is one of the largest of the parrot family.

- **Unlike most parrots**, the kea of New Zealand eats meat as well as fruit and insects. It feasts on carrion – animals that are already dead – and also hunts young shearwaters in their burrows.

- **Macaws** nest in tree holes high in rainforest trees. The female lays two eggs which her mate helps to incubate. The young macaws stay with their parents for up to 2 years

- **The little blue-crowned hanging parrot** gets its name from its strange habit of hanging upside down from a branch when at rest.

- **Macaws** swallow beakfuls of clay from riverbanks. The clay may help to protect the birds from the effects of some plants and seeds that they eat, many of which are poisonous to other creatures.

◀ *The male and female eclectus parrot have very different plumage. The male (here on the right) is bright green with a yellow bill, while the female is red with a blue belly and a black bill.*

▶ *With its bright red feathers, the scarlet macaw is one of the most beautiful of all the parrots. It can fly at up to 56 km/h as it searches the rainforest for fruit, nuts and seeds to eat.*

- **There are about 350 species** in the parrot group, including birds such as macaws, budgerigars, lories and cockatoos. They live in Central and South America, Africa, southern Asia and Australasia

- **As early as 400** BC, a Greek author wrote of owning a pet parrot – a bird that could speak words in both Indian and Greek!

...FASCINATING FACT...
The pattern of feathers on each side of the red-and-green macaw's face is unique – no two birds look identical.

Warblers

◄► The willow warbler (left) and the chiffchaff (right) look extremely similar. They can be told apart, however, by their different song patterns.

- **The willow warbler** is only 11 cm long, but flies all the way from northern Europe and Siberia to Africa to spend the winter – a distance of some 12,000 km.

- **The rarely seen grasshopper warbler** has an extraordinary whirring song and can 'throw its voice' like a ventriloquist.

- **The warbler family** has more than 380 species. Most live in Europe, Africa, Asia and Australasia, but there are a few species in North and South America.

- **Most warblers** are 9–16 cm long, but the two largest – the South African grassbird and the Australian songlarks – are up to 23 cm long.

- **The Aldabra warbler**, discovered in 1967, lives only on a small part of Aldabra Island in the Indian Ocean. It has not been seen since 1983, so may well be extinct.

- **Insects** are the main food of most warblers, but they also eat some fruits, berries and seeds.

- **The marsh warbler** can mimic about 80 other species.

- **Chiffchaffs and willow warblers** look almost exactly alike, but their songs are quite different.

- **The blackcap** lays 4–6 eggs in a neat, cup-shaped nest. Both parents incubate them for 10–15 days.

- **The tailorbird** makes a cradle like nest from two leaves which it sews together with plant fibres or spiders' webs.

▲ *At 19 cm long, the great reed warbler is larger than most European warblers.*

Manakins and cotingas

- **Manakins** are small birds that live in Central and South America. There are about 57 species.

- **Female manakins** do all the nesting work alone – they build the nest, incubate the eggs and care for the young.

▼ *Male cock-of-the-rocks have brilliant red heads and shoulders and perform complex display dances to females during the breeding season.*

- **The largest of the cotingas** is the Amazonian umbrellabird, which gets its name from the crest of feathers that hangs over its head.

- **The three-wattled bellbird** (cotinga family) is best known for its extremely loud call, which resounds through its jungle home.

- **Two of the most colourful South American birds** are the Guianan cock-of-the-rock, which is bright orange, and the Andean cock-of-the-rock, which is red (both cotinga family species).

- **Cocks-of-the-rock** perform remarkable courtship displays – up to 25 male birds leap and dance together, fanning their feathers and making loud calls.

- **The 65 or so cotinga species** live in the forests of Mexico, some Caribbean islands and Central and South America.

- **Fruit and insects** are the main foods of both manakins and cotingas.

- **The female cock-of-the-rock** makes a nest of mud and plants attached to a rock or cave wall, and incubates her eggs alone.

- **In his courtship display**, the male wire-tailed manakin brushes the female's chin with his long, wirelike tail feathers.

▲ *The little wire-tailed manakin lives in the lower levels of the Amazonian rainforest.*

Tyrant flycatchers

- **The tyrant flycatcher family** comprises between 370 and 395 species of birds. They range from northern Canada through the USA to the tip of South America.

- **Not all flycatchers** feed only on insects. The great kiskadee dives into water for fish and tadpoles, as well as catching flying insects in the air.

▲ *The tyrant flycatchers are the largest bird family in North and South America. Shown here are: (1) the buff-breasted flycatcher, (2) the lesser flycatcher and (3) the great-crested flycatcher.*

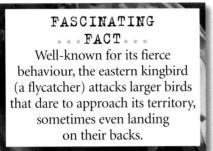

Well-known for its fierce behaviour, the eastern kingbird (a flycatcher) attacks larger birds that dare to approach its territory, sometimes even landing on their backs.

▶ *The vermilion flycatcher brings a flash of colour to the desert and dry scrub of the southwestern USA, Central America and tropical South America.*

- **The vermilion flycatcher** is one of the few brightly coloured flycatchers. The male has bright red plumage, which it shows off in his courtship display.

- **In 1976, ornithologists** – bird-watchers – in Peru found a previously unknown flycatcher, which they named the cinnamon-breasted tody-tyrant. It lives only in cloud forests on a few mountain peaks in Peru.

- **The royal flycatcher** is a plain, brownish bird, but it has an amazing crest of feathers on its head that it sometimes unfurls and shows off. Males have red crests and females yellow or orange crests.

- **Smallest of all the tyrant flycatchers** is the short-tailed pygmy tyrant, at only 6.5 cm long. It lives in northern South America.

- **The eastern phoebe** makes a nest of mud mixed with grass and plant stems. The female lays 3–7 eggs, and incubates them for 14–16 days. The young leave the nest when they are about 17 days old.

- **The boat-billed flycatcher** has a larger beak than other flycatchers, and eats frogs and other small animals, as well as insects.

- **Some flycatchers**, including the great crested flycatcher, line their nests with snakeskins that have been cast off.

Old World flycatchers

- **The spotted flycatcher** sits on a branch watching for insect prey, then darts out to catch it in mid-air – it has been seen catching one insect every 18 seconds.

- **The rufous-bellied niltava** lives and breeds in the Himalayas at altitudes of up to 2300 m.

- **The male pied flycatcher** may have two nests some distance apart, but he only helps rear the young in one of them.

- **There are 147 species of Old World flycatchers**. Some live in wooded parts of Europe, but they are more common in Asia, Africa and Australasia.

- **After a summer in Europe**, the red-breasted flycatcher flies to India and Southeast Asia for the winter.

- **The white-throated jungle flycatcher** is now very rare and lives only on two islands in the Philippines.

- **The female red-breasted flycatcher** makes a cup-shaped nest of moss, leaves, spiders' webs and plant down in which to lay her 5–6 eggs.

◀ *The spotted flycatcher lives in woodland, parks and gardens in Europe and parts of Asia and Africa.*

- **Male spotted flycatchers** bring all the food for their brood when they first hatch. Later, both parents feed the chicks.

- **Instead of catching all its food in the air**, the Australian flame robin often pounces onto its prey from a low perch.

- **In autumn and winter**, the pied flycatcher eats worms and berries as well as insects.

▲ *Some Old World flycatchers have dull brown plumage. This male narcissus flycatcher has a bright yellow breast, but the female is plainer.*

◄ *Old World flycatchers belong to the passerines (or songbird) group, but generally, they are not good singers and have a sharp, harsh call.*

59

Vireos and relatives

- **Plantcutters** get their name from their large, serrated beaks, used to chop leaves from plants.

- **The three species of plantcutter** live in southern South America. The birds are 17–20 cm long.

- **The sharpbill** of Central and South America picks tiny insects and spiders from leaves.

- **The 43 species of vireo** live in North, Central and South America, and range in size from 10–16 cm.

- **The black-capped vireo** usually attaches its nest to a forked twig. Both parents incubate the 3–5 eggs and feed the young.

- **Red-eyed vireo chicks** are naked and helpless when they hatch, but open their eyes after 4–5 days, and leave the nest after 12 days.

- **Insects** such as caterpillars and aphids are the main foods of vireos, but some species also eat fruit.

◀ *The red-eyed vireo breeds in North America in the summer.*

● **Vireos** take about a week to make their nest. The female makes a cup-shape of spiders' webs and silkworm threads around her body, and then adds plant material such as grass and moss to the nest.

● **When vireos were first named** in the 1800s, people thought they heard the word 'vireo', meaning 'I am green', in the birds' song. In fact most vireos are green.

● **The brown-headed cowbird** often lays its eggs in the nests of vireos, which sometimes throw out the cowbird's eggs.

▲▶ *Different species of vireo often live alongside each other in their forest habitats by feeding at different levels.*

61

Nuthatches and relatives

- **The red-breasted nuthatch** paints the entrance of its tree hole nest with sticky pine resin. This may stop insects and other creatures getting into the nest, but the birds also have to take care not to get their own feathers stuck.

- **The wallcreeper** is an expert climber and can clamber up steep cliffs and walls in its search for insect prey. It lives high in mountains such as the Alps and Himalayas.

- **The treecreeper** supports itself with its stiff tail feathers as it moves up tree trunks feeding on insects and spiders.

- **The 24 or so species of nuthatch** live in North America, Europe, north Africa, Asia and Australasia.

▲ *Most nuthatches stay in the same area all year round. It is only the red-breasted nuthatch that migrates seasonally.*

▶ *The common treecreeper lives in woodland, parks and gardens in Europe and Asia.*

- **The European nuthatch's 6–9 eggs** hatch after 14–18 days.

- **Insects and spiders** are the main food of nuthatches, but in autumn the birds store nuts and seeds for the winter.

- **There are seven species** of treecreeper, seven species of Australian creeper and two species of Philippine creeper.

- **The largest nuthatch** is the giant nuthatch, which is up to 20 cm in length.

- **The Kabylie nuthatch** was only discovered in 1975, on an Algerian mountain.

▶ *Clark's nutcracker is a mountain bird, but weather conditions and availability of food mean that it lives at a variety of altitudes.*

... **FASCINATING FACT** ...
Nuthatches are the only birds that can climb down trees head first, as well as up.

Mockingbirds and relatives

- **Mockingbirds** are so-called because they imitate the calls of other bird species – as many as 36 in all.

- **The alpine accentor** breeds high in the mountains, and has been seen nesting at 8000 m in the Himalayas.

- **As well as mockingbirds**, the 32 species in the family includes birds such as catbirds, thrashers and tremblers. They live in North and South America.

- **The brown trembler,** a resident of some Caribbean islands, gets its name from its habit of shaking its body from time to time.

- **The 13 accentor species** live in mountainous parts of northern Africa, Europe and Asia.

- **'Mimic of many tongues'** is the meaning of the northern mockingbird's scientific name, *Mimus polyglottus.*

◄ *The northern mockingbird is the best mimic in its family, usually copying the sounds made by other bird species.*

◀ *The catbird is a cousin of the mockingbird with its characteristic, mimicking song.*

> **FASCINATING**
> **. . . FACT . . .**
> The northern
> mockingbird
> can sing 200 songs,
> as well as mimicking
> pianos, frogs
> and humans.

- **The grey catbird** lines its cup-shaped nest of sticks, leaves and grasses with pine needles and down. The female lays 3–5 eggs, and incubates them for 12–13 days.

- **The brown thrasher** scatters dead leaves with its beak as it searches on the ground for its insect prey.

- **The catbird** gets its name from its strange, catlike call.

Shrikes and vangas

- **If it has plenty of prey**, such as lizards, frogs or insects, the northern shrike will store items for later by impaling them on a thorn bush or barbed wire fence.

- **Shrikes** are also known as 'butcher birds', because of their habit of storing prey on the thorns and barbs of trees and bushes.

- **The 14 species of vanga** live only on Madagascar and the neighbouring Comoros Islands.

- **The fiscal shrike** is very aggressive – it sometimes kills other birds.

- **During its courtship display**, the male puffback (a shrike) fluffs up the long feathers on its lower back like a powder puff.

- **There are about 65 species of shrikes** found in Africa, Europe, Asia and North America, as well as 72 species of cuckoo-shrikes and 9 species of helmet shrikes.

- **All shrikes** have powerful hooked beaks that they use for killing insects, lizards and frogs.

- **The call of the brubru shrike** sounds just like a phone ring.

- **The loggerhead shrike** makes a nest of twigs and grass in a thorny bush or tree, where the female incubates 5–7 eggs.

▲ *The sickle-billed vanga is named after its long, curved beak.*

66

● **The sickle-billed vanga** uses its long, curved beak to probe bark for insects. It hangs upside down by its claws while it feeds.

◄▲ *Shrikes are keen predators. Some species create a kind of 'larder', using thorns or wire, on which to store prey.*

67

Pittas and relatives

- **Bright red, green or yellow eyes** characterize the 15 colourful species of broadbill, which live in parts of tropical Africa and Southeast Asia.

- **The brightly coloured pittas** live in Africa, Southeast Asia and Australia. 'Pitta' is an Indian word meaning 'bird' – it was first used in the 1700s.

- **The four species of asity** are found only in Madagascar.

- **Most broadbills** feed on insects, which they catch in the air. Some also eat lizards and frogs.

- **The 24 or so species of pitta** range in size from 15–25 cm.

▶ *The hooded pitta (front) and red-bellied pitta live in tropical rainforests.*

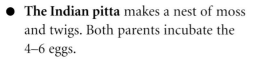

- **The Indian pitta** makes a nest of moss and twigs. Both parents incubate the 4–6 eggs.

- **The wattled false sunbird** (asity family) gets its name from its long, sunbird-like beak. Like the sunbirds, it takes nectar from flowers.

- **The green broadbill** hangs its nest from a vine and covers it with lichen and spiders' webs.

- **Pittas are said to have the best sense of smell** of any songbird. This may help them find worms and snails in the dim light of the forest floor.

▲ *Broadbills inhabit the tropics eastwards from central Africa. They can be up to 28 cm in length and are skilled nest-builders.*

... FASCINATING FACT ...
Rainbow pittas put wallaby droppings in and round their nests to disguise their own smell and keep tree snakes away from their eggs.

69

Buntings and tanagers

- **The little snow bunting** breeds in northern Greenland, further north than any other bird.

- **One tanager, the glossy flowerpiercer**, has a hooked, up-curved beak that it uses to pierce the bases of tubular flowers so it can feed on the nectar inside.

- **The 240 species in the tanager family** include flowerpiercers, honeycreepers and euphonias. All live in North and South America.

- **The male scarlet tanager** has bright red feathers in the breeding season, but in autumn his plumage changes to olive-green, similar to the female.

- **The western tanager** lines its nest of twigs and moss with fine roots and animal hair. The female incubates 3–5 eggs.

- **Some tanagers follow columns of army ants** in forests, and snap up the insects that flee the ants' path.

- **Seeds** are the main food of the dark-eyed junco (bunting family), although it does eat a few spiders.

- **The woodpecker finch** (a bunting) uses a fine twig or cactus spine as a tool to winkle out insects from holes.

- **The 13 species of finch** (bunting family) in the Galapagos Islands are probably all descended from the same ancestor, but have evolved different beak shapes and feeding habits depending on their environment.

- **The Galapagos finches** gave Charles Darwin important evidence for his theory of evolution.

▶ Tanagers are a colourful group of birds that live in the mainly tropical forests of South America.

71

Bowerbirds

- **Male bowerbirds** build bowers of twigs and other plant material to attract females. They decorate their creations with berries and shells, and some even perform dances in front of their bowers.

- **The Vogelkop gardener bowerbird** builds a hutlike structure big enough for a person to crawl into.

- **Male bowerbirds' bowers** are not built as a place for the female to lay eggs and rear young. The females build their own, more practical nests.

> ... FASCINATING FACT ...
> The satin bowerbird decorates its bower with blue flowers, feathers, and even bottletops.

▼ *Male bowerbirds build complex structures called bowers in order to attract females.*

▼ *The golden bowerbird is the smallest of its family, but makes a bower of 3 m high!*

- **The forests of New Guinea** and northern and eastern Australia are home to the 18 or so species of bowerbird.

- **At about 36 cm long**, the great grey bowerbird of northern Australia is the largest of the family.

- **Bowerbirds** feed on fruit, berries, seeds, insects and other small creatures.

- **A female bowerbird** cares for her 1–3 chicks alone.

- **The male regent bowerbird** paints its bower yellow using a mix of spit and the juice of crushed leaves.

- **Catbirds** are members of the bowerbird family. They get their name from their catlike calls.

Antbirds and tapaculos

- **Antbirds** follow columns of army ants as they march over the forest floor, perching just above the ground to seize other insects as they flee from the ants' path.

- **The 230 or so species of antbird** live in Mexico, Central and South America.

- **The 30 species of tapaculos** are insect-eating birds that live in the cool mountain forests of South America or in dry scrubland.

- **Antbirds** mate for life.

- **During the courtship ritual** of the ocellated antbird, the male presents the female with an item of food.

- **Antbirds have white spots** on their back feathers, which they use to signal warnings to each other. They show the spots in particular patterns according to the message – like a sort of Morse code.

◀ *Female antbirds are often brownish or greenish in colour. Males usually have dark grey plumage with white markings.*

- **Antbird species** range from 10–38 cm long, and have differently shaped beaks to suit their food.

- **Some larger species of antbirds** have a special 'tooth' inside the beak that helps them chew food.

- **Most antbirds** do not fly much and have poorly developed wings, but their legs are strong, for running and perching.

▼ *Lines of army ants lead tropical antbirds to their food.*

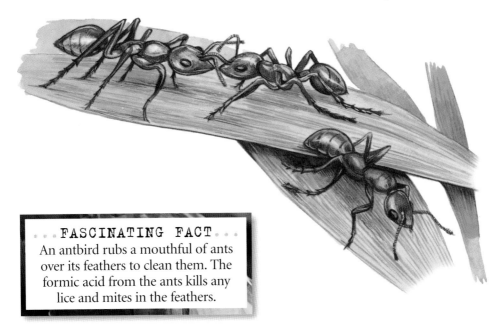

...FASCINATING FACT...
An antbird rubs a mouthful of ants over its feathers to clean them. The formic acid from the ants kills any lice and mites in the feathers.

Finches and relatives

- **The crossbill** gets its name from its crossed beak, specially shaped for extracting seeds from pine cones.

- **The beaks** of some crossbills cross to the left, while those of others cross to the right.

- **Canaries** were first domesticated in the early 16th century, from the island canary of the Canary Islands, the Azores and Madeira.

- **The male American goldfinch** brings the female food while she incubates the 4–6 eggs.

- **The akiapolaau** – a Hawaiian finch – hammers on bark to find insect prey with the short, straight, lower part of its unique beak, and extracts them with the longer, curved upper part.

- **The kernels** of cherry stones and olive stones are a favourite food of the strong-beaked hawfinch.

- **The goldfinch** uses its slender beak like tweezers to take seeds from between the spines of a teasel head.

- **The iiwi**, a Hawaiian finch, has a long, curved beak used for drinking nectar from flowers.

- **Siskins and goldfinches** have long been popular as cage birds, and are now rare in many areas.

▶ *The colourful goldfinch, a common sight in the English countryside, has a red face, beige body and yellow wing flashes.*

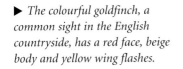

▲ *The distinctive, pink-breasted bullfinch.*

. . . **FASCINATING FACT** . . .
Although the hawfinch weighs
only 50 g, its beak can exert a
pressure of 45 kg.

77

Thrushes and dippers

- **The wheatear breeds** in the Arctic, but in autumn flies some 3200 km to Africa, where it spends the winter.

- **The dipper** is the only type of songbird to live in and around water – it can swim underwater and even walk along streambeds as it searches for insect prey.

▼ *Dippers make their homes near water. When they walk on the stream bed, they hold onto stones to keep themselves from surfacing.*

- **The familiar orange-red breast** of a robin indicates that the bird is at least 2 months old.

- **More than 300 species** of thrush are found nearly all over the world.

- **Best known for its beautiful song**, the nightingale sings during the day as well as at night.

- **The female blackbird** makes a cup-shaped nest of plant stems, grass, twigs and roots. The 4–5 eggs hatch after 11–17 days.

- **The five species of dipper** live in Europe, Asia and parts of North and South America.

- **The dome-shaped nests** of dippers usually have an entrance over running water.

- **The American robin** – the largest of the North American thrushes – lives both in cities and mountains.

- **Blackbirds** were taken to Australia and New Zealand in the 19th century. Their songs are now clearly different to blackbirds living in Europe.

▶ *The European robin is Britain's national bird.*

Wrens and babblers

- **The white-necked rockfowl** (babbler family) makes a mud nest on the roof of caves. It sometimes builds onto old wasps' nests.

- **The cactus wren** builds its nest among the spines of the chola cactus. Few enemies will brave the spines to steal the wren's eggs or young.

- **At about 23 cm long**, the black-capped donacobious of South America is the largest of the wren family.

- **The only species** of the babbler family to live in North America is the wren-tit, while 256 species are found in Asia, Africa and Australasia.

- **The tuneful song** of the red-billed leiothrix (babbler family) makes it a popular cage bird in China.

- **Although common in west Africa**, the pale-breasted thrush-babbler is so good at hiding on the forest floor, where it searches for insects, that it is rarely seen.

◀ *The cactus wren makes several decoy nests in different cactus plants to fool predators.*

- **A male wren** courts a mate by building up to 12 nests. The female chooses one in which to lay her eggs.

- **The nothern (or winter) wren** usually lays 5–8 eggs, and incubates them for 14–17 days. The young stay in the nest for 20 days.

- **Brightly coloured patches** of bare skin on the head are a distinguishing feature of rockfowl (babbler family).

- **Most wrens** live in North and South America. Only the northern wren lives in Europe, Asia and Africa.

▲ *Babbler males and females raise their young together.*

81

Sunbirds and relatives

- **The 115 or so species of sunbird** live in tropical parts of Africa, Asia and Australia.

- **The Kauai o-o**, a honeyeater, was thought to be extinct, but in 1960 some birds were found, and there is now a very small protected population.

- **The flowerpecker family** contains about 58 species living in parts of Asia, Southeast Asia and Australia.

- **At about 23 cm long**, the Sao Tomé giant sunbird is the largest of its family. It uses its hooked beak to dig into the bark of trees for insects.

- **Sunbirds** use their long, slender beaks and tubular tongues to extract sweet liquid nectar from flowers.

- **Female sunbirds** make purse-shaped nests for their 2–3 eggs, which hatch after 13–15 days.

- **Honeyeaters** are the most important flower pollinators in Australia. The brushlike tip on the honeyeater's tongue helps it to extract flower nectar.

- **The crested berrypecker** (flowerpecker family) has a habit of rubbing its plumage with crushed flower petals.

▶ *Sunbirds feed from tropical flowers. They often hover as they do so, but cannot fly backwards like hummingbirds.*

82

● **The tui** (honeyeater family) of New Zealand is also known as the parson bird, because it has a distinctive bib of white feathers at its throat.

▼ *The bluish flowerpecker is a distinctive blue colour with a short beak and cropped tail feathers.*

...**FASCINATING FACT**...
The mistletoe bird (flowerpecker family) swallows mistletoe berries whole, digesting only the flesh and not the seeds.

Lyrebirds and relatives

- **One of the biggest of all the songbirds**, the superb lyrebird has an extraordinary lyre-shaped tail, with feathers more than 50 cm long.

- **The rifleman**, one of the three species of New Zealand wren, lays eggs that are about 20% of her body weight. She and the male recruit helpers to bring food to their young.

- **The two species of scrub-bird** live in Australia, where they feed on insects, lizards and frogs.

- **In its loud song**, the lyrebird may imitate other birds, barking dogs, chainsaws and even passing trains.

- **The female lyrebird** builds a domed nest, usually close to the ground. Her one chick stays with her for 8 months or more.

◀ The lyrebird spends most of its life on the ground searching for insects.

- **The rufous scrub-bird** spends most of its time on the ground and rarely flies.
- **The two species of lyrebird** live in dense mountain forest in southeastern Australia.
- **Named after the small island** in Cook Strait where it lived, the Stephen Island wren was killed off by the lighthouse keeper's cat. It may have been the only flightless songbird.
- **A full-grown rufous scrub-bird** is 16–18 cm long and weighs about 30 g.
- **Young male superb lyrebirds** do not grow their lyre-shaped tails until they are 3 or 4 years old.

▶ *The rifleman is a common sight on the North and South islands of New Zealand.*

Ovenbirds and relatives

- **The nest of the firewood-gatherer** (ovenbird family) looks like a bonfire. A group of birds make the nest together and sleep in it during the winter.

- **The red-billed scythebill** (a woodcreeper) has a long, curved beak for delving deep into rainforest plants such as ferns and bromeliads to search for insects.

- **Ovenbirds** live in the forests, mountains and semideserts of Mexico, Central and South America.

- **Woodcreepers** often nest in old woodpecker nests.

- **The common miner** (an ovenbird) digs a 3-m long burrow with a nest chamber at the end, where it raises its chicks and roosts for the rest of the year.

▶ *The rufous hornero is the national bird of Argentina.*

- **Des Murs' wiretail** (an ovenbird) has only six tail feathers, four of which may be three times the length of the body.

- **The 50 or so species of woodcreeper** live in forests and woodland in Mexico, Central and South America.

- **Insects and spiders** hiding among the densely packed leaves of bromeliads may be extracted by the long, probing beak of the long-billed woodcreeper.

- **The campo miner** (an ovenbird) nests in a very particular place – an old armadillo burrow.

▶ *The red-billed scythebill is easily distinguished by its long, down-curved beak.*

.....FASCINATING FACT.....
The rufous hornero's mud-and-straw nest is shaped like an old-fashioned clay oven.

87

Old World sparrows

- **The house sparrow** originally came from Southwest Asia, but has spread throughout the world. It feeds mainly on seeds, but also eats some insects and is happy to eat scraps put out on bird tables.

- **Chestnut sparrows** drive other birds from their nests and use the nests themselves, instead of making their own.

- **The snow finch** lives high in mountain ranges and makes its nest on mountain ledges at altitudes of 5000 m.

◀ *The mountain-dwelling snow finch is one of the highest-living of all birds.*

> **...FASCINATING FACT...**
> Sparrows like to bathe and splash in water, and will even bathe in snow in winter.

- **All the house sparrows** in the USA are descended from a few birds that were released in Central Park, New York, in 1850.

- **House sparrows** generally have two broods a year of 4–7 eggs each.

- **The desert sparrow** makes a nest of grass and twigs, often in a wall, and lays 2–5 eggs.

▶ *There may now be as many as 150 million house sparrows in the USA.*

- **Most sparrows** are about 14–18 cm long and have brownish or grey plumage.

- **The 40 or so species of Old World sparrow** live in Europe, Africa and parts of Asia, though some have been introduced elsewhere.

- **House sparrows** rarely nest away from human habitation.

Drongos and relatives

- **The huia**, a species of wattlebird, has not been seen since 1907 and is probably extinct. It was noted for having a different shaped beak in males and females – the male's was straight and strong, the female's slender and curved.

- **The greater racquet-tailed drongo** has two long, wirelike tail feathers with twisted tips that make a humming noise as the bird flies.

- **The pied currawong** (Australian butcherbird family) attacks other birds and takes their young from their nests.

- **The 25 species of Old World oriole** live in Europe and parts of Asia, Africa and Australia. They are mainly tree-dwellers, feeding on insects, seeds and fruit.

- **There are two surviving species** of the wattlebird family – the kokako and the wattlebird, both of which live in New Zealand and rarely fly.

▲ *Drongos are aggressive predators. They mainly feed on insects but sometimes rob birds of their prey!*

- **The golden oriole** makes a neat, cup-shaped nest that it binds to two supporting twigs. It lays 3–4 eggs.

- **Australia and New Guinea** are home to the 10 species of insect-eating bell-magpies.

- **Australian mud-nesters** work together to build nests of mud on the branches of trees.

- **The figbird** (oriole family) is a forest fruit-eater, but is now also common in towns.

- **Wood swallows**, found in Australasia and Southeast Asia, feed mostly on insects, but also drink nectar.

◀ *The greater racquet-tailed drongo has a plume of feathers on its head and long, vinelike tail streamers.*

91

Waxwings and relatives

- **The waxwing** gets its name from the red markings like drops of wax at the tips of its wing feathers.

- **Palmchats** nest in palm trees. One nest may house 30 pairs of birds, each with its own tunnel entrance to the outside.

- **The silky flycatcher** feeds mostly on mistletoe berries, passing out the seeds.

- **The bohemian waxwing** makes a nest of twigs, moss and grass, usually in a conifer tree. The female incubates 4–6 eggs, while the male keeps her fed.

◀ *Bohemian waxwings will strip a bush clean of its berries before moving on.*

- **Adult cedar waxwings** store berries in their crops, or throat pouches, and regurgitate them for their young.

- **The female silky flycatcher** builds a nest, but it is the male who incubates his mate's eggs.

> **· · ·FASCINATING FACT· · ·**
> When courting, a male bohemian waxwing gives the female a gift – a berry or ant larva.

- **Adult waxwings** eat mainly berries, but feed their young on insects for the first two weeks of their lives.

- **The single species of palmchat** is found on the islands of Haiti and the Dominican Republic in the Caribbean.

- **Cedar waxwings** have been seen sitting in rows on a branch passing a berry from one bird to the next until one of them swallows it!

▼ *There are three species of waxwings. All are very sociable, tree-dwelling birds.*

Wood warblers and icterids

- **The crested oropendola**, an icterid, weaves a hanging nest that may be up to 1 m long. The birds nest in colonies, and there may be as many as 100 large hanging nests in one tree.

- **Like the cuckoo**, the female brown-headed cowbird lays her eggs in the nests of other birds. She lays about 12–15 eggs a year.

- **Kirtland's warbler** has very specialized breeding needs – it nests only around jack pine trees that are up to about 6 m tall.

- **The 114 species of wood warbler** live in North, Central and South America.

- **The bobolink** breeds in southern Canada and the USA and migrates to South America for the winter – the longest migration journey of any icterid.

▶ *The male northern oriole, also known as the Baltimore oriole, has vibrant orange and black plumage. The female is a duller olive-brown with orange or whitish underparts.*

- **Great-tailed grackles** (icterid family) are big, noisy birds that scavenge on rubbish as well as feeding on insects, grain and fruit. They are common in towns and villages.

- **The Baltimore oriole** is the state bird of Maryland, USA. A song named after the bird was written by Hoagy Carmichael in the 1930s.

- **Male icterids** are generally much larger than females. The male great-tailed grackle is as much as 60% heavier than the female.

- **The yellow warbler** lays 4–5 eggs in a nest of bark and plant fibres made in a tree.

- **The largest of the 92 species** of icterid is the olive oropendola, which measures 52 cm in length.

◀ *The yellow warbler can be found from chilly Alaska to tropical South America.*

95

Bulbuls and relatives

- **The bearded greenbul** lives in African rainforests and has a beautiful whistling call that it uses to keep in touch with others of its species in the dense jungle.

- **Despite its small size**, the red-vented bulbul is an aggressive bird. In Asia, people sometimes bet on a male bird to win a fight against another male.

- **The yellow-vented bulbul** makes a nest of twigs, leaves and vine stems, often in a garden or on a balcony. Both parents incubate the 2–5 eggs and care for the young.

- **There are about 120 species of bulbul** found in Africa and southern Asia, usually in forests, although some bulbuls have adapted to built-up areas.

> ...FASCINATING FACT...
> When courting, the male common iora fluffs up its feathers, leaps into the air and tumbles back to its perch again.

▶ *The fairy bluebird spends most of its time in trees, feeding on nectar and ripe fruit, especially figs.*

- **Bulbuls** range in size from 14–23 cm, and eat mainly insects and fruit.
- **The two species of fairy bluebirds** live in Asia, feeding on fruit, nectar and some insects.
- **Leafbirds** lay 2–3 eggs in a cup-shaped nest made in the trees.
- **The common iora** (a leafbird) scurries through trees searching the leaves for insects. It also sometimes eats mistletoe and other berries.
- **Male fairy bluebirds** have bright blue upperparts. Females are a dull greenish-blue with dark markings.

▲ *The red-whiskered bulbul is a common sight in gardens and cultivated land in India, south China and Southeast Asia.*

Tits

- **The blue tit** is only 10–11 cm long, but lays as many as 15 eggs – more than any other bird that feeds its young.

- **The largest of the tits** is the Asian sultan tit, at about 22 cm long and 30 g in weight. It is twice the size of most other tits.

- **The penduline tit** makes an amazing nest woven from plant fibres and suspended from the end of a twig. The walls of the nest may be 2.5 cm thick.

- **There are about 50 species of true tits** found in Europe, Africa, Asia and North America. In addition, there are seven species of long-tailed tits and 10 species of penduline tits.

- **The black-capped chickadee** gets its name from its call, which sounds like a 'chick-a-dee-dee', and is one of the most complex of any bird songs.

◀ *Great tits normally lay large clutches of eggs in nest boxes or trees. Their young are independent in two to four weeks.*

- **The female great tit** lays 8–13 eggs, each of which is about 10% of her body weight.

- **Great tits** hatch blind and helpless, and are fed by their parents for about 3 weeks. The parents may make 1000 feeding trips a day to the young.

- **The long-tailed tit** makes its nest from feathers and moss that it collects – one nest may contain as many as 2000 feathers in all.

- **The long-tailed tit** is only about 14 cm long, and more than half of its length is its tail feathers.

...**FASCINATING FACT**...
The willow tit may bury up to
1000 nuts and seeds a day, to eat
later when food is scarce.

▶ Agile little blue tits and their relatives can often be seen clinging to wire bird feeders in gardens during the winter.

Birds of paradise

- **Birds of paradise**, of which there are about 44 species, live only in New Guinea and northeastern Australia.

- **The king of Saxony bird of paradise** has two 50 cm head plumes decorated with small, sky-blue squares, so unusual-looking they were first thought to be fake.

- **The magnificent riflebird** gets its name from its loud whistling call, which sounds like a passing bullet.

- **Most female birds of paradise** make a cup or dome-shaped nest and lay 1–2 eggs.

> ...**FASCINATING FACT**...
> The tail feathers of the male
> ribbon-tailed bird of paradise are
> up to 1 m long.

▲ *The blue bird of paradise is a rare member of this exotic family*

▶ *The male king bird of paradise uses his long, wirelike tail feathers in his courtship display.*

- **During courtship**, the blue bird of paradise hangs upside-down from a branch with his splendid blue feathers and tail plumes spread over his head.

- **Fruit and insects** are the main foods of the birds of paradise. Some also eat leaves and buds.

- **New Guinea tribesmen** traditionally wear bird of paradise feathers in their head-dresses.

- **During the early 19th century**, 100,000 bird of paradise skins were sold each year in Europe for hat and dress decorations.

- **The first bird of paradise skins** brought to Europe from New Guinea did not have feet, so some people thought the birds never landed.

101

Starlings

- **The male wattled starling** loses his head feathers in the breeding season. Scientists investigating cures for human baldness are researching the bird's ability to regrow its head feathers each year.

- **When kept in captivity**, hill mynahs mimic human speech, but wild birds do not imitate the calls of other bird species, only the calls of other hill mynahs.

- **The largest starlings** are up to 43 cm long and weigh just over 100 g.

- **European starlings** feed their young on caterpillars, earthworms and beetle grubs, and may make 400 feeding trips a day.

- **Male starlings** bring fresh green leaves to the nest while the eggs are incubating. It is believed that the leaves release a substance that deters bird parasites such as lice.

- **The Brahminy starling** has a brush-like tip on its tongue, used for collecting pollen and nectar.

- **There are about 113 species** of starling in Europe, Africa and Asia. Starlings have also been introduced into Australasia and North America.

> ... FASCINATING FACT ...
> In some cities, flocks of up to one million starlings gather for the night.

◀ *The male starling has glossy, iridescent plumage. The female is much plainer, with brownish feathers.*

▲ *The splendid starling of Africa has beautiful bluish-green feathers and bright yellow eyes.*

- **Some 100 years ago**, 60 pairs of European starlings were released in New York. Fifty years later, starlings were one of the most common birds in the USA.
- **Locusts** are the favourite food of the rose-coloured starling. Large flocks fly to wherever they are plentiful.

103

Monarchs and relatives

- **Monarch flycatchers** feed mainly on insects, darting out to catch them in the air and then taking them back to a perch to eat.

- **The male African paradise** flycatcher's tail feathers are up to 20 cm long – much longer than its body.

- **Only seven Chatham Island robins** (Australasian robin family) were thought to exist in 1976, but a breeding programme using the Chatham Island tit to foster eggs has helped increase the population.

- **There are about 90 species** of monarch flycatchers. They live in wooded areas in Africa, Southeast Asia, Australia and some Pacific islands.

▶ *Monarch flycatchers are good parents, building a nest in the fork of a tree and sharing responsibility for incubating eggs and rearing their young.*

- **The yellow-breasted boatbill**, a monarch flycatcher, has a broad beak with a hooked tip, which it uses to pick small insects off leaves.

- **Smallest of the Australasian robin family** is the rose robin, at 10 cm long and weighing only 10 g.

- **The black-naped blue monarch** lays 3–4 eggs in a nest of grass and bark bound together with spiders' webs. The nest is usually built on a forked branch.

- **According to aboriginal folklore**, the willie wagtail (a fantail), is a gossipy bird that spreads secrets.

- **The pied fantail's beak** is ringed with bristles that may help the bird to trap insect prey.

▲ *The paradise flycatcher makes a neat nest of plant roots held together with spiders' webs on a slender branch or twig.*

．．．FASCINATING FACT．．．
Fantails are so-named because they continually fan their long tails from side to side.

105

Hawks and harriers

- **The female sparrowhawk** is almost twice the size of the male. At breeding time she defends the nest while the more agile male brings the family food.

- **The marsh harrier** flies close to the ground searching for mice, rats, frogs, rabbits and even fish. When it sights prey, it swoops down, seizes the victim in its sharp talons and tears it apart with its beak.

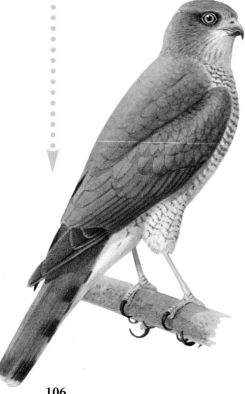

- **Tiny spines** on the underside of the black-collared hawk's toes help it catch and hold slippery fish prey.

- **The African harrier hawk** likes to feed on baby birds. It has long, double-jointed legs that allow it to reach into other birds' nests and grab the chicks.

- **There are about 66 species** of hawks and harriers, including goshawks and sparrowhawks.

- **Young goshawks** first leave the nest at about 40 days old and start to fly at about 45 days. By 50 days or so they can hunt for themselves, and by 70 days they can manage without their parents.

◀ *The sparrowhawk preys mostly on other birds, ranging in size from tits to pheasants.*

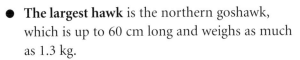
- **The largest hawk** is the northern goshawk, which is up to 60 cm long and weighs as much as 1.3 kg.

- **Fledgling goshawks** 'play' as a way of practising their hunting skills.

- **At least 95%** of the northern harrier's diet is mice.

- **The smallest hawk** is the African little sparrowhawk, which is only about 25 cm long.

▶ *Red-tailed hawks, like all birds of prey, are excellent fliers. They move gracefully and swoop down on unsuspecting prey with sudden bursts of speed.*

107

Falcons

- **The peregrine** (a type of falcon) is the fastest bird, diving through the air at 180 km/h to catch prey.

- **The peregrine's hunting** technique is so exacting that only one in ten attacks is successful.

- **At up to 60 cm long**, the gyr falcon is the largest of the falcon family, and can catch ducks and hares.

▼ *Like other birds of prey, the gyr falcon has exceptionally sharp eyesight which helps it find prey.*

- **The common kestrel** hovers above the ground on fast-beating wings while it searches for small mammals.

- **Falconets and pygmy falcons** are the smallest birds of prey. The Philippine falconet is only 15 cm long.

- **Falcons have adapted well** to city life – kestrels hover above rubbish bins to watch for mice, and peregrines dive down between New York skyscrapers.

- **Eleonora's falcon** is named after a 14th-century Sardinian princess, who brought in laws to protect it.

- **The earliest known records** of falconry come from 2nd-century BC China.

- **In winter**, both male and female kestrels spend about a quarter of their day hunting. But when the female is incubating eggs, the male hunts for longer.

> ...FASCINATING FACT...
> Kestrels can see ultra-violet light,
> which reflects off the urine a
> rodent uses to mark its tracks.

▶ *The peregrine kills with its talons and rips prey apart with its sharp, hooked beak.*

109

Buzzards, kites and osprey

- **Bees and wasps**, their larvae and even their nests are the main food of honey buzzards, which remove the stings from adult insects before eating them.

- **The snail kite's hook-tipped beak** is perfectly shaped for extracting the soft flesh of snails from their shells.

- **One of the most common** of all birds of prey is the black kite, which lives throughout most of Europe, Africa, Asia and Australia.

- **The black kite** is a scavenger as well as a hunter, taking food from dustbins and even market stalls!

> ...FASCINATING FACT...
> The osprey was described by
> Aristotle as early as 350 BC in his
> Natural History.

◀ The osprey's body measures 55–58 cm long, and it has an impressive 1.6-m wingspan. The females are slightly larger than the males.

- **When fishing**, the osprey plunges into water feet first and grasps its slithery prey with its spine-covered feet.

- **The red kite** often takes over the old nest of a raven.

- **The rough-legged buzzard** is common over open tundra in the far north. It preys on rodents and rabbits.

- **A buzzard** can spot a rabbit popping up out of its burrow from more than 3 km away.

- **Male ospreys** feed the whole family once the chicks have hatched.

▼ *With its sharp, curved beak and piercing red eyes, the kite is an impressive sight.*

Owls

- **Owls range** in size from the least pygmy owl, at only 12–14 cm long, to the Eurasian eagle owl, at 71 cm.

- **The burrowing owl** nests in burrows in the ground, either digging its own with its strong claws, or taking over the burrows of other animals such as prairie dogs.

- **The soft, fluffy edges** of an owl's feathers help to reduce flight noise, so it can hunt almost silently.

- **The brown fish owl** has bare legs and feet – feathers would get clogged with fish scales.

- **The 150 or so species of owl** live in most parts of the world except the far north, New Zealand and Antarctica.

▼ *Pel's fishing owl lives along riverbanks in parts of southern Africa.*

- **About 80 species** of owl hunt mostly at night.

- **Some Native Americans** believed that owls were the souls of people, and so should never be harmed.

- **The female barn owl** lays 4–7 eggs, often in a tree hole.

- **Female owls** are usually larger than males.

- **Owls swallow their prey**, such as mice and insects, whole.

▶ An owl's eyes are large and forward-facing to enable it to judge distances accurately when flying and hunting prey.

115

Snake and sea eagles

- **The bald eagle** performs an amazing courtship display, in which the male and female lock their claws together and tumble through the air to the ground.

- **The short-toed eagle** kills a snake with a bite to the back of the head, instantly severing the backbone.

- **The white-tailed sea eagle** snatches fish from the water using its sharp, powerful talons.

- **The bald eagle** was chosen as the national emblem of the USA in 1782, and appears on most of the gold and silver coins in the USA.

▶ *The distinctive, adaptable bateleur eagle is widespread across Africa in grassland, mountain and desert regions.*

- **Spikes** on the underside of its toes help the African fish eagle hold onto its fish prey. It also catches birds, terrapins and baby crocodiles.

- **Bald eagles** are not really bald. They have white feathers on their heads, which may make them appear bald from a distance.

- **The bateleur**, a snake eagle, may fly as much as 300 km a day in search of food.

- **Snake eagles** do eat snakes, and have short, strong toes ideal for tackling their writhing victims.

- **The name** 'bateleur' means 'tumbler' or 'tightrope walker' in French, and refers to the rocking, acrobatic movements that the bird makes in flight.

- **There are only about 40 pairs** of the Madagascar fish eagle left in the world.

▼ *Fish eagles use their lethally sharp talons to snatch fish from the water.*

True and harpy eagles

- **The most powerful of all eagles,** the South American harpy eagle hunts prey that may weigh more than itself, such as large monkeys and sloths.

- **The Philippine eagle** is one of the rarest of all birds of prey. Twenty years ago there were only about 200 birds. Now they are strictly protected, and there is a captive breeding programme to increase numbers.

- **The golden eagle** makes a bulky nest of sticks and branches (called an eyrie) that may measure as much as 2 m high and 1.5 m across.

- **A harpy eagle** weighs over 8 kg, has a wingspan of more than 2 m, and talons the size of a bear's claws.

> **...FASCINATING FACT...**
> A eaglet weighs only 85 g when it hatches, but by the time it reaches adulthood the bird weighs about 7 kg.

- **True eagles** are also known as booted eagles, because their legs are covered with feathers down to their toes.

- **Verreaux's eagle** lays two eggs, but the first chick to hatch usually kills the younger chick.

- **At up to 96 cm long,** the martial eagle is the largest African eagle. It feeds on mammals such as hyrax and young antelope, and on other birds, including guineafowl and even storks.

- **A young martial eagle** is fed by its parents for about 60 days, by which time is has a full covering of feathers and is able to tear up prey for itself.

- **The golden eagle** usually has a hunting territory of about 260 sq km.

▼ *Golden eagles lay two eggs, but one chick usually dies. At first the mother keeps the surviving chick warm while the male finds food, but as the chick grows larger, both parents are kept busy supplying it with food.*

Hooked beak
for tearing
apart its prey

Large eyes –
the eagle has
excellent eyesight

Tapering wing feathers
increase lift so the eagle
can soar for long periods

Long curved talons

117

New World vultures

- **There are seven species of New World vultures** in North and South America. Like Old World vultures, their diet includes carrion.

- **New World vultures** do not build nests, but simply lay their eggs on the ground or on a cliff ledge. The parent birds feed their young on regurgitated food.

- **Unusually colourful** for a bird of prey, the king vulture has bright red, orange and yellow bare skin and wattles on its head.

- **The king vulture** has a particularly good sense of smell, and can find carrion even in dense rainforest.

- **Pairs of turkey vultures** raise their young together. Both parents help to incubate the eggs (usually 1–3) for up to 41 days.

▲ *Vultures have bald heads and necks so that they can reach right inside a carcass when they feed.*

- **Black vulture chicks** are looked after by both parents. They do not fly until they are 11 weeks old.

- **Vultures** can go for weeks without food. When they do find carrion, they eat as much as possible.

- **King vultures** have stronger beaks than other New World vultures, and are able to tear apart large animals.

- **The last wild California condors** were captured for captive breeding. By 1998 there were 150 birds, 35 of which were released into the wild. Today, there are over 170, with 50 flying free in the wild.

- **The largest of all birds of prey** is the Andean condor, with a wingspan of more than 3 m.

▲ *The Andean condor is a metre or more in length with black and white plumage and distinctive wing feathers which are splayed out like fingers during flight.*

119

Old World vultures

- **There are about 15 species** of Old World vulture living in southern Europe, Africa and Asia.

- **Unlike most birds of prey,** the palm-nut vulture is mostly vegetarian. Its main food is the husk of the oil palm fruit, although it also eats fish, frogs and other small creatures.

- **The Egyptian vulture** steals birds' eggs. It cracks the eggs by dropping them on the ground or throwing stones at them.

- **Most vultures are scavengers** rather than hunters – they feed on the carcasses of dead animals.

- **The lack of feathers** on a vulture's head means that it does not have to do lots of preening after it has plunged its beak deep into a carcass to feed.

◀ *The bearded vulture, unlike other vultures, has face and neck feathers.*

- **Different species** of vulture eat different parts of a body – bearded vultures even eat the bones of their prey.

- **In hot weather,** some vultures cool down by squirting urine onto their legs – which can't smell nice!

- **The female white-backed vulture** lays one egg in a large stick nest made high in a tree. She incubates the egg for 56 days, being fed by the male. Both parents feed and care for the chick.

- **The lappet-faced vulture** is the largest vulture in Africa – it measures about 1 m long and has a huge 2.8 m wingspan. It also has a bigger beak than any other bird of prey.

▶ *This Egyptian vulture is about to break open a thick-shelled ostrich egg with a stone so that it can eat the contents. The vulture also eats carrion – several birds may be seen circling above a dead or dying animal when they find one.*

. . . **FASCINATING FACT** . . .
The bearded vulture drops bones from a great height to smash them. It then swallows the bone fragments, which are broken down by powerful acids in its stomach.

Hooked beak for pecking scraps of meat from bones

Stone raised to throw at egg to break it open

121

Avocets and relatives

- **The seven species of stilts** and avocets are all long-legged wading birds with long, slender beaks.

- **Female pheasant-tailed jacanas** mate with up to 10 males in one breeding season. The males incubate the eggs and care for the young.

- **The long, curved beak** of the pied avocet turns up at the end. The bird sweeps this strange tool through mud or shallow water to find worms and shrimps.

- **The black-winged stilt** has extremely long, bright pink legs that allow it to wade in deeper water than other stilts as it searches for worms and shellfish.

... FASCINATING FACT ...
The American jacana has extremely long toes and claws that spread the bird's weight, allowing it to walk on floating water-lily leaves.

◀ *The pied avocet has a distinctive, upturned beak for feeding in its marshland home.*

- **Jacanas** range in size from 16–53 cm long.
- **Avocets** nest in a hollow in the ground, lined with dead leaves. Both partners incubate the 3–5 eggs.
- **Young avocets** can run soon after hatching, and can fend for themselves after 6 weeks.
- **Young jacanas** often hide underneath floating leaves if danger threatens.
- **If a male pheasant-tailed jacana** thinks his eggs are in danger, he may move them one at a time, holding them between its breast and throat.

▶ *The jacana is sometimes called the 'lily-trotter' because of its unique way of moving over the leaves of water plants.*

Plovers and lapwings

- **The wrybill**, a New Zealand plover, has a unique beak that curves to the right. The bird sweeps its beak over sand to pick up insects.

- **If a predator** comes near a killdeer's nest, the bird moves away, trailing a wing to look as though it is injured. The predator, seeing what it thinks is an easy victim, follows the killdeer which, once far enough away, flies off.

- **Kentish plover chicks** have markings like the stones and pebbles of their nest site. If danger threatens, the chicks flatten themselves on the ground and are almost impossible to see.

- **There are 60 or so species** of plovers and lapwings (also known as peewits) around the world.

- **Female dotterels** lay clutches of eggs for several males, which incubate the eggs.

- **To attract females**, the male lapwing performs a spectacular rolling, tumbling display flight in the air.

- **Spur-winged plovers** are often seen close to crocodiles in Africa and Asia – they may feed on small creatures that the crocodiles disturb.

- **Most plovers** feed on insects, shellfish and worms.

- **Golden plovers** have been recorded flying at more than 113 km/h.

> **...FASCINATING FACT...**
> Many plovers pat the ground with their feet to imitate the sound of rain. This attracts worms to the surface, where they are snapped up.

▶ *The wrybill breeds on New Zealand's South Island, but overwinters on North Island.*

Pelicans

- **The great white pelican** catches about 1.2 kg of fish a day in its large throat pouch.

- **The brown pelican** dives from a height of 15 m above the water to catch fish below the surface.

- **Great white pelican breeding colonies** may number as many as 30,000 pairs of birds.

- **There are seven species of pelican.** Most live and feed around fresh water, but the brown pelican is a seabird.

▲ *A great white pelican comes in to land on the water.*

- **One of the largest pelicans** is the Australian pelican, which is up to 180 cm long and weighs about 15 kg.

- **The white pelican** lays 1–2 eggs in a nest mound on the ground. Both parents help to incubate the eggs and care for the young.

- **Pelican chicks** are able to stand at 3 weeks old and can fly at 7–10 weeks old.

- **In heraldry**, a pelican is shown pecking its breast to feed its young on its blood. This may stem from the bird's habit of resting its beak on its breast.

- **White pelicans** work as a group to herd fish into a shoal by swimming around them in a horseshoe formation. Then they scoop up pouchfuls of fish with their large beaks.

- **In flight**, a pelican flaps its wings 1.3 times a second. This is one of the slowest wingbeat speeds, when actively flying, of any bird.

▼ *Pelicans are often found in large colonies, particularly during the breeding season.*

Storks

- **In tropical areas**, storks' nests perched high on buildings can get very warm, so parents cool their young by regurgitating a shower of water over them.

- **The huge beak** of the whale-billed stork, or shoebill, is 23 cm long and 10 cm wide. It uses it to catch lungfish, young crocodiles and turtles.

▲ *Like other wading birds, storks have long, spindly legs, plump bodies and long bills for catching fish.*

- **The white stork** has long been a symbol of fertility in Europe. Parents used to tell their children that new babies were brought by a stork.

- **The 17 species of stork** live in North and South America, Europe, Africa, Asia and Australia.

- **Marabou storks** often scavenge on rubbish tips.

- **The openbill stork's beak** meets only at the tip. This helps it to hold its favourite food – large snails.

- **The tail feathers of marabou storks** were once used to trim hats and dresses.

- **When the wood stork's** partly open beak touches a fish under water, it snaps shut in 25 milliseconds – this is one of the fastest reactions of any animal.

▲ *The saddlebill stork of southern Africa is easily recognized by its large red, yellow and black bill.*

- **Male and female white storks** take turns to incubate their clutch of 3–5 eggs. When the partners change shifts, they perform a special bill-clattering display.

- **The adjutant stork** is named after the adjutant army officer, because of its stiff, military-style walk.

129

Cranes and trumpeters

- **The whooping crane** is one of the world's most endangered birds, with only about 300 surviving in 2001.

- **The crowned crane**, which has a fine crest of yellow feathers, performs a spectacular courtship display that involves leaping 2 m into the air.

- **The three species of trumpeter** live in tropical rainforests. All make a loud trumpeting call – hence their name.

- **In China and Japan** the crane symbolizes long life and good luck.

- **At about 1.5 m long**, the Sarus crane of India, Southeast Asia and northern Australia is one of the largest members of the crane family.

- **The limpkin** is a relative of the cranes and the only member of its family. It has a long, curved beak, which it uses to remove snails from their shells.

◀ *The handsome crowned crane lives in Africa, usually around swamps and marshland.*

▼ *Cranes fly with their neck stretched forwards and their legs held straight out beyond the short tail.*

- **Trumpeters** spend most of their time on the ground in search of fruit, nuts and insects, but they roost in trees.

- **The sandhill crane** makes a nest of plant material on the ground. The female lays two eggs, which both parents help to incubate. Soon after hatching, the young leave the nest.

- **Siberian cranes** have been known to live more than 80 years – one captive male even fathered chicks at the age of 78!

- **The 14 or so species of crane** live all over the world, in North America, Africa, Europe, Asia and Australia.

Ibises and relatives

▲ *The scarlet ibis is one of the most striking birds in the world with its deep red plumage and black tail feathers.*

● **The ibis** was a symbol of the god Thoth in ancient Egypt, and appears in many paintings and carvings. Mummified ibises have also been discovered – as many as 500,000 in one tomb.

● **The spoonbill's beak** has a spoon-shaped tip that it uses to search shallow water for fish and small creatures.

● **At 1.4 m in height** and weighing about 4 kg, the greater flamingo is the largest of the 5 species of flamingo.

● **The greater flamingo** has a wingspan of 140–165 cm.

● **The flamingo** feeds by forcing mud and water through bristly plates at each side of its beak with its tongue. Tiny creatures, algae and other food particles are trapped and swallowed.

● **Until their beaks have developed fully,** young flamingos feed on a 'milky' substance from their parents' throats.

● **The 31 species of ibis and spoonbill** live in North and South America, southern Europe, Asia, Africa and Australia, often in wetlands.

● **The glossy ibis** makes its nest in a reedbed or tree, and lays 3–4 eggs. The female does most of the incubation, but the male helps to rear the young.

● **Young flamingos** have grey feathers at first. Adult birds get their pink colour from pigments in the algae that they eat.

...FASCINATING FACT...
Ibises and spoonbills are an ancient group of birds – fossils of their ancestors have been found that date back 60 million years.

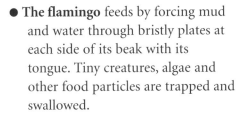

Beak for filtering food from water

▶ *The greater flamingo lives in huge flocks around lakes and deltas in Europe, Asia, parts of Africa, the Caribbean and Central America. It may live to be at least 50 years old.*

Long neck allows the bird to feed in deep water

133

Herons and bitterns

- **There are about 60 species** of heron and bittern.

- **The largest of the heron family** is the goliath heron of Africa and southwest Asia – it measures 1.5 m long.

- **The loud booming call** made by the male bittern in the breeding season can be heard up to 5 km away.

- **The great blue heron** makes a platform nest of twigs, often high in a tree. The four eggs take 25–29 days to hatch.

- **Special feathers** on the heron's breast and rump crumble into a powdery substance. The bird rubs this into its plumage to remove dirt and fish slime.

▲ *The great egret catches fish and shellfish in shallow waters.*

> ...FASCINATING FACT...
> The green-backed heron of Japan tempts fish with bits of 'bait' such as bread or feathers.

- **The white feathers** of the great egret were popular hat decorations in the late 1800s – more than 200,000 birds were killed for their feathers in a single year.

- **Like most herons**, the grey heron feeds on fish and frogs, which it catches with swift stabs of its beak.

- **Cattle egrets** nest in colonies – there may be more than 100 nests close together in one tree.

- **When hunting**, the black heron holds its wings over its head like a sunshade. This may help the bird spot fish, or the patch of shade may attract fish to the area.

▶ *Herons are swift, efficient hunters, using their long, sharp beaks to stab at fish.*

Rails and bustards

- **The weka** is a flightless rail that lives in New Zealand. Its diet includes seeds, fruit, mice, eggs and insects, and it also scavenges in rubbish bins.

- **Female great bustards** are much smaller and lighter than males, weighing only about 5 kg.

- **The world's smallest flightless bird**, the Inaccessible Island rail, weighs only 35 g – about the same as a small tomato. It lives on Inaccessible Island in the South Atlantic Ocean.

- **There are more than 130 species of rails** found all over the world, including many small islands. The family includes moorhens, coots and crakes, as well as rails.

▶ *The kori bustard is one of the heaviest of all flying birds. It lives on the African plains, eating insects and soft vegetation.*

▼ *The great bustard, with its 2.5 m wingspan, lives on the plains, steppes and farmland of Europe and Asia, feeding mainly on insects and plants.*

- **The takahe**, a large flightless rail, is now extremely rare and lives only in South Island, New Zealand.
- **The 22 species of bustard** live in Africa, southern Europe, Asia and Australia.
- **Fights between Asian watercocks** (a type of rail) are staged for sport in some parts of Asia.
- **Coots** are the most aquatic of all the rails. They dive in search of plants and water insects to eat.
- **The female moorhen** makes a nest of dead leaves at the water's edge. The male helps incubate the 5–11 eggs.

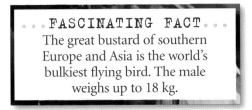

. . . FASCINATING FACT . . .
The great bustard of southern Europe and Asia is the world's bulkiest flying bird. The male weighs up to 18 kg.

Finfoots and relatives

- **The sunbittern** gets its name from the rich red-orange markings on its wings.

- **The sungrebe** (finfoot family) has an unusual way of caring for its young. The male bird carries his chicks in two skin pouches beneath his wings while they complete their development, even flying with them.

- **The only species in its family**, the sunbittern lives in jungles and swamps in Central and South America.

- **The kagu** is a flightless bird that lives solely on the Pacific island of New Caledonia.

- **Finfoots are aquatic birds** that feed in the water on fish, frogs and shellfish. There is one species each in Afric, Southeast Asia and Central and South America.

◄ Finfoots lay 2–7 eggs in a nest made among reeds or near water.

▶ *A sunbittern spreads its wings, showing off its beautiful plumage.*

- **The two species of seriema** live in South America. They eat snakes, banging their heads on the ground to kill them.

- **Seriemas** can fly, but prefer to escape danger by running fast over the grassy plains where they live.

- **Much of the kagu's habitat** on the island of New Caledonia has been destroyed by nickel mining, and the bird is now very rare.

- **The sunbittern** lays two eggs in a tree nest made of leaves and plant stems. Both parents take turns to incubate the eggs and care for the chicks.

- **The sungrebe and finfoots** have lobed feet, which help them swim.

139

Ducks

- **The female eider duck** lines her nest with soft down feathers that she pulls from her breast. Humans use the feathers too, to make quilts and sleeping bags.

- **Torrent ducks** live by fast-flowing streams in South America's Andes mountains. When new ducklings hatch, they leap straight into the swirling waters.

- **There are more than 100 duck species**, living all over the world, except Antarctica.

- **Steamer ducks** get their name from their habit of paddling over water with their wings as well as their feet, at speeds of up to 28 km/h.

- **Ducks** have been domesticated for more than 2000 years for their meat and eggs.

- **Ducks** feed on fish, shellfish, leaves and seeds.

- **Like cuckoos**, the black-headed duck lays its eggs in the nests of other birds, such as herons.

▲ *The male mandarin duck shows off his elaborate, colourful plumage in special courtship displays.*

- **The merganser** has a serrated beak like the blade of a bread knife, to help it hold slippery fish.

- **The wood duck** was hunted nearly to extinction in the 19th century for the male's colourful feathers, which were used as ornate fishing flies and hat decorations.

- **The red-breasted merganser** is one of the fastest-flying birds. It can reach speeds of more than 65 km/h – and possibly even 100 km/h.

▼ *Ducks are highly sociable birds and can adapt to a variety of aquatic environments.*

Geese and swans

- **Whooper, trumpeter and mute swans** are among the heaviest flying birds, weighing up to 16 kg.

- **Snow geese** breed in the Arctic tundra, but fly south to spend the winter months around the Gulf of Mexico – a journey of some 3500 km.

- **The black swan** makes a nest of sticks and other plant material in shallow water and lays up to six eggs. Both parents help to incubate the eggs.

- **Geese** feed mostly on leaves, and can eat as many as 100 blades of grass in one minute.

- **Tundra swans mate for life**, returning year after year to the same nesting site. They usually make their nest on marshland and lay 3–5 eggs.

- **Although quieter than other swans**, the mute swan is not really mute, but makes many snorting and hissing calls.

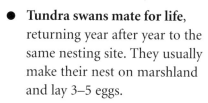

◀ *The Hawaiian goose was saved from extinction by a captive breeding programme.*

142

- **The Hawaiian goose** is the world's rarest goose. Fifty years ago there were only about 30 left. Now it is protected and numbers are increasing.

- **Red-breasted geese** often make their nests near those of peregrines and buzzards. This gives them protection, and they don't seem to get attacked by the birds of prey.

- **Male swans** are known as 'cobs', females as 'pens' and baby swans are called 'cygnets'.

... **FASCINATING FACT** ...
Bar-headed geese have been seen flying near the top of Mount Everest, at 8848 m high.

▼ *Swans generally mate for life.*

Sandpipers

- **Coasts and marshes** are the home of the 88 or so species of sandpiper, which include curlews, snipe and phalaropes. Most have long beaks and long legs.

- **The western curlew** plunges its long, curved beak into soft coastal mud to find worms and clams.

- **As it dives towards Earth**, air rushing through the outermost tail feathers of the European snipe makes a sound called 'drumming'.

- **Sandpipers** range in size from the eastern curlew, at about 66 cm long, to the least sandpiper, at 11 cm.

- **Once the dowitcher's four eggs** have hatched, feeding the chicks is the sole responsibility of the male.

◀ *The curlew's long legs are ideal for wading over marshland.*

144

- **Unusually for birds**, female phalaropes are more brightly coloured than males. The female lays several clutches of eggs, leaving the male parent of each clutch to do all the caring for the young.

▶ *The turnstone breeds on Arctic coasts but flies further south for the winter.*

- **The turnstone** is so-named because it turns over stones on the beach whilst searching for shellfish and worms.

- **In the breeding season**, male ruffs grow amazing feathers around the head and neck, and dance in groups to attract females.

Terns and skimmers

- **The noddy**, a species of tern, gets its name from its habit of nodding its head during its courtship display.

- **The black skimmer's beak** has a flattened lower part that is longer than the upper part. The bird flies over water with the lower part of its beak just below the surface, ready to snap up prey.

- **The 42 or so species of terns** are found all over the world, mostly along coasts.

▼ *Skimmers are so-called because of the way they 'skim' the water for fish with their sensitive beaks*

- **Arctic terns** are long-lived birds, known to survive to 27 – and sometimes even 34 – years of age.

- **Most terns** eat fish, squid and shellfish, but marshland terns also eat insects and frogs.

- **At up to 59 cm long**, the Caspian tern is the largest of the terns, and one of the most widespread.

- **The fairy tern** does not make a nest. Instead, it balances its one egg on a tree branch and manages to sit on it without knocking it off.

- **Most terns mate for life**. Even if they don't stay together all year round, pairs meet up when they return to breeding sites.

- **There are only three species of skimmers.** All live in areas of tropical Africa, Southeast Asia and North and South America.

▲ *The Arctic tern has a long, forked tail, short red legs, pointed beak and a covering of black feathers on its head.*

Gulls and relatives

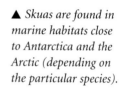

▲ *Skuas are found in marine habitats close to Antarctica and the Arctic (depending on the particular species).*

- **The great skua** is a pirate – it chases other birds and forces them to give up their prey in mid air.

- **The snowy sheathbill** scavenges for food on Antarctic research bases, and also steals eggs and chicks from penguin colonies.

- **There are about 48 species** of gull found on shores and islands all over the world.

- **Arctic glaucous and ivory gulls** sometimes feed on the faeces of marine mammals.

- **At up to 79 cm long**, the great black-backed gull is the giant of the group. The little gull is one of the smallest, at 28 cm long.

- **The Arctic explorer** James Clark Ross discovered Ross's gull in the 19th-century.

- **Skuas, also called jaegers,** usually lay two eggs in a shallow, moss-lined nest on the ground. Both parents incubate the eggs and feed the young, which can fend for themselves by after about seven weeks.

- **The kittiwake** spends much more time at sea than other gulls, and usually only comes to land in the breeding season. It has very short legs and very rarely walks.

- **Herring gulls** have learned that they can find food in seaside towns, and many now nest on roofs instead of cliff ledges.

- **The south polar skua** lays two eggs, but the first chick to hatch usually kills the second.

◀ *The sheathbill is an aggressive scavenger. It lives and breeds solely in Antarctica and its immediate regions, such as the Falkland Islands and the very bottom of South America.*

▶ *Like most gulls, the kittiwake has startling white plumage with black markings – here, on its tail feathers.*

149

Shearwaters and petrels

- **The shearwater's legs** are placed far back on its body, making it an expert swimmer, but preventing it from standing up properly. It moves awkwardly on land and has to launch itself from a tree into the air.

- **Unlike most birds**, shearwaters and petrels have a good sense of smell. They have long, tube-shaped nostrils on the tops of their beaks.

- **Shearwaters and petrels** are not tuneful birds, and at night the colonies make a very loud, harsh noise.

- **The 56 or more species** in the shearwater family include petrels, fulmars and prions. They range from the Antarctic to the Arctic.

◀ As storm petrels hunt for fish, they 'step' over the water's surface.

150

- **Largest of the shearwater family** are the giant petrel which at 99 cm long are almost the size of albatrosses.

- **Fish and squid** are the main food of shearwaters, but giant petrels also feed on carrion, and can rip apart whales and seals with their powerful beaks.

- **The manx shearwater** lays one egg in a burrow. The male and female take turns at incubating it and feeding one another.

- **Young shearwaters** are fed on a rich mixture of regurgitated fish and squid, and may put on weight so quickly that they are soon heavier than their parents.

- **Prions feed on tiny plankton**, which they filter from the water through comblike structures at the sides of their beaks.

▶ *Manx shearwaters nest in colonies of thousands of birds on offshore islands or isolated cliff tops.*

....FASCINATING FACT....
To defend themselves, shearwaters can spit out food and fish oil to a distance of 1 m.

151

Oystercatchers and relatives

- **The oystercatcher** uses its strong, bladelike beak to prise mussels off rocks and open their shells.

- **Oystercatcher chicks** stay with their parents for up to one year while they learn how to find and open shellfish.

- **The Egyptian plover** (courser family) buries its eggs in sand and leaves them to be incubated by the warmth of the sun. The parents sit on the eggs at night and if the weather is cool.

- **The cream-coloured courser** has pale, sandy feathers that help to keep it hidden in its desert home.

- **The 17 species** in the courser and pratincole family live in southern Europe, Asia, Africa and Australia.

- **The common pratincole** nests on sand or rocks, and lays 2–4 mottled, well-camouflaged eggs. The parents take turns to incubate the eggs for 17–18 days.

▶ *The common pratincole feeds on insects and will follow swarms of locusts.*

152

- **The nine species in the thick-knee family** include the stone curlew and the dikkop. These long-legged birds usually feed at night on insects, worms and shellfish.

- **The thick-knees** get their common name from the knobbly joints on their legs – actually between the ankle and shin bones.

- **If the Egyptian plover's** chicks get too hot, the parent birds soak their own belly feathers with water and give their young a cooling shower.

- **The pygmy seed-snipe** of southern South America blends in with the plains landscape so well that it is almost invisible when it crouches on the ground.

▶ *The common oystercatcher breeds in Europe and Asia, but spends the winter in South Africa and southern Asia.*

153

Auks

- **The Atlantic puffin's colourful beak** is striped red, yellow and grey blue, and can hold 12 or more fish.

- **The ancient murrelet** is so-named because it develops fine white feathers on its head in the breeding season. These are said to look like the white hairs of an elderly person.

- **The common guillemot nests** on narrow cliff ledges. Its eggs are pointed, so that if they get knocked, they roll in a circle and do not fall off.

- **The guillemot** can dive in water to a depth of 180 m as it hunts.

- **The auk family** includes 22 species of diving birds, including auks, guillemots, puffins and razorbills. They live in and around the North Pacific, Atlantic and Arctic Oceans.

- **The common guillemot** is the largest of the auks, at about 45 cm long and 1 kg in weight. The least auklet is the smallest auk, at 16 cm long and 90 g.

▲ *The female guillemot lays her one egg on the ground, where both parents share incubation duties.*

- **Common guillemots** nest in colonies of thousands, with as many as 70 pairs occupying 1 sq m.

- **The little auk** nests in a cliff crevice and lays 1–2 eggs, which both parents incubate.

- **Auk eggs** are reputed to taste good, and have long been collected and eaten by humans.

... **FASCINATING FACT** ...
The puffin flies at up to 64 km/h, with its wings beating 300–400 times a minute.

▶ *The red, yellow and blue bill of the puffin fades after the breeding season when the colourful outer scales are shed.*

155

Large seabirds

▼ *Squid is the main food of the wandering albatross, but it will also snatch fish waste thrown from fishing boats. An expert glider, it can sail downwind from a height of about 15 m to just above the water's surface, before turning back into the wind to be blown upwards.*

- **The wandering albatross** has the longest wings of any bird – from tip to tip they are an incredible 3.4 m.

- **The white-tailed tropicbird** is noted for its amazing tail streamers, which measure up to 40 cm long.

- **The male frigatebird** has a bright red throat pouch that he inflates during courtship to attract females.

- **The wandering albatross** often flies 500 km in a day, soaring over the ocean in search of food.

- **The pirates of the bird** world are frigatebirds, which often chase other seabirds in the air and harass them into giving up their catches.

- **Frigatebird chicks** depend on their parents for longer than most birds. They start to fly at about 6 months, but continue to be fed until they are one-year old.

- **The five species of frigatebird** fly over tropical areas of all oceans. They spend most of their lives in the air, rarely descending to land on water.

● **The three species of tropicbird** are all expert in the air and can dive into the sea to find prey, but cannot walk on land. With their legs set far back on their bodies, they are only able to drag themselves along.

● **The wandering albatross** can only breed every other year. It incubates its eggs for 11 weeks, and the chicks do not fly until they are about 40 weeks old.

Long wings for gliding on the wind

.... FASCINATING FACT ....
A wandering albatross chick may eat as much as 100 kg of food during the time it is being fed by its parents.

▲ *When courting a mate, the male frigatebird clatters his beak and flaps his wings, as well as inflating his red throat pouch into an eye-catching balloon.*

Penguins

- **Not all of the 18 species** of penguin live in Antarctica. A few species live around Australia and South Africa, and there is even one resident in the Galapagos Islands on the Equator.

- **Penguins** have wings, but cannot fly. They spend as much as 85% of their time in water, where they use their wings like flippers to help push themselves through the water.

- **The king penguin** has been known to dive down to 250 m in search of prey.

- **An emperor penguin** may travel at least 900 km on a single feeding expedition.

... FASCINATING FACT ...
The male emperor penguin incubates his mate's eggs for 60 days, eating nothing and losing as much as 45% of his body weight.

An emperor penguin stands about 110 cm high

Emperor penguin chick

▲ *An emperor chick spends the first 2 months of its life on its parent's feet, protected from the cold by a pouch of skin. If it falls off, it freezes to death in seconds.*

▲ *Emperor penguins have highly streamlined bodies, allowing them to dive to depths of 275 m when they hunt. They can stay underwater for several minutes, using their strong flippers to propel them forward.*

- **Like many other penguins,** gentoos nest in a simple scrape on the ground, but they surround it with a ring of pebbles. A courting gentoo shows its mate an example of the sort of pebbles it will provide.

- **The emperor penguin** keeps its egg warm on its feet, where it is covered by a fold of skin. The temperature there stays at a constant 36°C, despite the freezing surroundings.

- **Penguins** eat fish, squid and shellfish. They have spiny tongues to help them hold on to slippery prey.

- **A dense covering** of three layers of feathers keeps penguins warm. An emperor penguin has about 12 feathers in each sq cm of its body.

- **Penguins** usually swim at 5–10 km/h, but can reach speeds of up to 24 km/h.

159

Divers and grebes

- **The great crested grebe** is best known for its amazing courtship dance, during which male and female perform a series of movements in water and exchange pieces of weed.

- **At 90 cm long,** the white-billed diver is the largest of the four species of diver.

- **The short-winged grebe** lives on lakes high in the mountains of Peru and Bolivia, and cannot fly. It basks in the sun to warm its body up after the cold nights.

- **Divers** feed only on fish, which they catch underwater. The great northern diver can dive as deep as 20 m or more below the water's surface.

- **In the 19th century,** the breast feathers of grebes were used to make muffs to keep ladies' hands warm.

- **There are about 20 species of grebes** (three flightless). They live near freshwater lakes and marshes.

...FASCINATING FACT...
Grebes have up to 20,000 feathers
to keep their bodies warm and dry
as they dive for food.

◀ *The great crested grebe lives in parts of Europe, Asia, Africa and Australasia.*

- **Divers** are so specialized for diving and swimming that adult birds cannot walk upright on land.

- **Grebes** feed on fish, insects and shellfish. They also swallow moulted feathers, which may help them to regurgitate waste such as fish bones and keep their guts free of parasites.

- **The great crested grebe** makes a nest of water plants floating near the water's edge. It lays 3–6 eggs, which both male and female incubate.

▲ *Blacknecked grebes make floating nests in marshy or freshwater lake areas.*

161

Cormorants and anhingas

◀ *Anhingas have slim, streamlined bodies and long, pointed beaks for spearing fish.*

- **The four species of anhinga or darter** all live in freshwater in tropical parts of the world. They are all are expert underwater hunters.

- **The flightless cormorant** lives on two of the Galapagos Islands. Its tiny wings are useless for flight, but it is an expert swimmer.

- **The feathers of cormorants** and darters lack waterproofing and quickly get soaked through. This makes the birds heavier in water and better able to dive for fish.

- **After diving for food**, cormorants stand on a rock with wings outstretched to dry.

- **In parts of Asia**, fishermen use cormorants to catch fish – the birds dive for the fish but do not swallow them.

- **Cormorant** colonies may number 100,000 birds or more. Their droppings, known as guano, are collected and used as fertilizer.

> **FASCINATING FACT**
> Cormorants can dive to an incredible 50 m or more in their hunt for fish.

- **The biggest species of cormorant**, the great cormorant, is up to 1 m long.

- **A great cormorant** eats about 15% of its body weight in fish a day. That's like an adult human eating more than 80 hamburgers a day.

- **The American darter**, or snake bird, swims with its neck held in a snakelike curve above the water's surface.

◄ *Cormorants have a characteristically kinked neck, enabling them to jab at fish with lightning speed. They are expert swimmers and divers but are slow and clumsy on land.*

163

Gannets and boobies

- **The gannet** plunges 30 m or so through the air and dives into the water to catch prey such as herring and mackerel.

- **A specially strengthened skull** helps cushion the impact of the gannet's high-speed dive into water.

- **Boobies** were given their common name because they were so easy for sailors to catch and kill.

- **The male blue-footed booby** attracts a mate by dancing and holding up his brightly coloured feet as it struts about.

- **The gannet** usually lays just one egg, which both partners help to incubate for 43–45 days. They feed their chick with regurgitated food for up to 13 weeks.

▲ *Gannets are expert divers and are common in North Atlantic and Mediterranean regions.*

- **There are three species of gannet** and six species of booby. Boobies generally live in tropical and subtropical areas, while gannets live in cooler, temperate parts of the world.

- **When a gannet comes** to take its turn incubating the egg, it presents its mate with a piece of seaweed, which is added to the nest.

- **Young gannets** and boobies are kept warm on their mother's feet for their first few weeks.

164

- **Boobies** spend the majority of their time at sea, only landing to breed and rear their young.

- **At up to 86 cm long** and with a wingspan of 152 cm, the masked booby is the largest of the boobies.

▲ *Rarer blue-footed boobies usually feed close to the seashore, while the more common red-footed booby tends to venture further out to sea.*

Mesites and relatives

- **Mesites are thrushlike birds** that search for insects on the forest floor. They do have wings, but rarely fly.

- **There were three species of mesite** in Madagascar, but two have not been seen for years and may be extinct.

- **The 15 species of buttonquail** live in parts of Europe, Africa, Asia, Australia and some Pacific islands, usually on grassland. Although they look like quails, they are not related.

- **Shy little birds,** buttonquails lurk among low-growing plants feeding on seeds and insects.

- **The female buttonquail** is larger than the male. She mates with several males and leaves each to incubate the clutch of eggs and rear the young.

◀ The little buttonquail lives in southern Europe, Africa and parts of Asia. It is 13–15 cm long.

- **Buttonquails** are sometimes known as hemipode, or half-footed, quails, because they lack rear toes.

- **The plains-wanderer** lives on the dry plains of central Australia. If in danger, it stays very still.

- **Plains-wanderers** are now rare because so much of the grassland where they live and feed has been cleared for agriculture. There may be fewer than 8000 left in the wild.

▲ *White-breasted mesites are a vulnerable species – they are exclusive to the island of Madagascar and their natural habitat is under threat.*

- **The female plains-wanderer** lays four eggs, usually in a nest made in a hollow in the ground, but it is the male that incubates the eggs and rears the young.

- **Buttonquail** young can fly two weeks after hatching, and start to breed when only 4–5 months old.

167

Ostriches and emu

- **The ostrich** is the largest of all birds alive today. It stands 2.5 m tall and weighs about 130 kg – more than twice as much as an average human.

- **The male emu** incubates his mate's clutch of eggs for eight weeks, during which time he does not eat or drink. He lives on the stores of body fat that he has built up during the previous months.

- **In Southwest Asia**, the shells of ostrich eggs are believed to have magical powers. For this reason, they are sometimes placed on the roofs of houses as protection from evil.

> **FASCINATING FACT**
> The ostrich cannot fly, but is a very fast runner. It can speed along at 60 km/h – as fast as a racehorse.

- **Ostriches** don't really bury their heads in the sand. But if a female is approached by an enemy while sitting on her nest on the ground, she will press her long neck flat on the ground, to appear less obvious.

- **The largest bird** in Australia is the emu, which measures 2 m tall and weighs as much as 45 kg. Like the ostrich, it cannot fly.

- **An ostrich feather** was used as a symbol of justice in ancient Egypt.

- **Seeds, fruits, flowers and plant shoots** are the emu's main sources of food, but it also eats some insects and small animals.

- **The male ostrich** makes a shallow nest on the ground and mates with several females, all of whom lay their eggs in the nest. The chief female incubates the eggs during the day, and the male takes over at night.

- **Ostrich chicks** have many enemies, including jackals and hyenas, and only 15% are likely to survive until their first birthday.

▼ *The ostrich lives in Africa in dry grassland areas, where it often has to run for long distances in search of food.*

The male has black feathers on its back; females and young birds have brown feathers

The long, flexible neck is bare skinned

Long, strong legs for running

Pheasants and relatives

- **Domestic chickens** are descended from the red jungle fowl, which was first domesticated 5000 years ago. The jungle fowl still lives wild in Southeast Asia.

- **All 49 species of wild pheasant** are from Asia, except the Congo peafowl, which was first discovered in a Central African rainforest in 1936.

- **To attract females**, the male great argus pheasant dances and spreads out his enormously long wing feathers, like glittering fans.

- **The peacock's** wonderful train contains about 200 shimmering feathers, each one decorated with eyelike markings. When courting, he spreads the train and makes it 'shiver' to attract a female.

- **The Himalayan monal pheasant** spends some of the year above the tree line, where it has to dig in the snow with its beak to find insects and other food.

▶ *The peafowl is a native of India, Sri Lanka and Pakistan, but it has been introduced in many areas throughout the world. Only the male (the peacock) has the spectacular tail, which does not reach its full glory until the bird is about 3 years old. It may continue to grow for another 2–3 years.*

- **The male pheasant** mates with several females, each of which lays up to 15 eggs in a shallow scrape on the ground. The females incubate the eggs and care for the young by themselves, with no help from the male.

- **Most pheasants** nest on the ground, but the five species of tragopan, which live in tropical forests in Asia, nest in trees, often taking over the old, abandoned nests of other birds.

- **The common pheasant** comes from Asia, but is now common in Australia, North America and Europe, where it is shot for sport.

- **In ancient Rome**, peacocks were roasted and served in their feathers as a great delicacy.

▶ *The male common pheasant is a beautiful bird with iridescent plumage on its head, bright red wattles and sometimes a white neck ring. Originally from Asia, this pheasant has been introduced in Europe and North America, where it is very common.*

> ···**FASCINATING FACT**···
> The crested argus has the largest, longest tail feathers of any bird, at up to 170 cm long and 12 cm wide.

173

Turkeys and grouse

- **Male wild turkeys** of the USA, Mexico and Central America can weigh up to 8 kg.

- **At 87 cm long**, the western capercaillie is the biggest of the 17 species of grouse. The female is only 60 cm long.

- **In winter**, the spruce grouse feeds mainly on the buds and needles of pine trees.

- **An adult turkey** has approximately 3500 feathers.

- **The 17 species of grouse** live in North America, Europe and northern Asia.

- **Wild turkeys** are not fussy eaters. They feed on a variety of seeds, nuts, berries, leaves, insects and other small creatures.

- **To attract females** and challenge rival males, the ruffed grouse makes a drumming sound with its wings.

▲ *The plumage of female gamebirds like this spruce grouse often seems very dull in comparison to that of the splendid male.*

> ...FASCINATING FACT...
> The heaviest ever domestic
> turkey weighed 39 kg – as much
> as a 12-year old child.

- **At the start of the breeding season**, foot-stamping dances are performed by groups of male prairie chickens at their traditional display areas.

- **The ruffed grouse lays 9–12 eggs**. When the young hatch, the female shows them where to find food.

▲ *Wild turkeys usually feed on the ground, but they are strong flyers over short distances.*

Megapodes and guans

- **The 12 species of megapodes** are ground-living birds found in Australia and some Pacific islands.

- **The mallee fowl** (a megapode) lays her eggs in a huge mound of rotting leaves and sand, which acts as an incubator. The mound can be up to 11 m across and 5 m high.

- **The male mallee fowl** checks the temperature of his nest mound with its beak and keeps it a constant 33°C by adding or removing material.

- **Mallee fowl chicks** must dig their way out of their nest mound, and are able to fly a few hours later.

▼ *The male mallee fowl keeps a constant watch on his nest.*

- **To attract females**, as it flies the male crested guan flaps his wings briefly at more than twice the normal speed, making a whirring sound.

- **One megapode in Tonga** makes a nest of hot volcanic ash, which keeps its eggs warm.

- **The 45 species of guan and curassow** live from the southern USA to northern Argentina.

- **The great curassow** is 95 cm long and weighs 4.8 kg.

- **True to its name**, the nocturnal curassow comes out at night to sing and feed on fruit.

- **The plain chachalaca** (curassow family) lays three eggs in a nest made of sticks and lined with leaves and moss.

- **Now rare**, the white-winged guan lives in the Andean foothills, feeding on fruit, berries, leaves and insects.

▶ *The curassow is a ground-dwelling forest bird, feeding on seeds, berries and small animals.*

Cassowaries and kiwis

- **There are three species of kiwi**, found only in New Zealand. All are flightless birds that live in burrows.

- **The female dwarf cassowary**, or moruk, is an extremely dangerous bird and will attack anything that comes near its nest with its 10-cm long claws.

- **The three species of cassowary** live in rainforests in New Zealand and northeastern Australia.

- **Largest of its family is the brown kiwi**, which is about 55 cm long and weighs up to 3.5 kg.

- **Only the kiwi** has nostrils at the end of its beak.

> ...**FASCINATING FACT**...
> A kiwi lays the largest eggs for its size of any bird – each egg weighs 25% of its body weight. Females lay up to 100 in a lifetime.

- **The kiwi** is the national symbol of New Zealand, appearing on stamps, coins and banknotes.

- **Cassowaries** in Australia are known to eat the fruits of 75 different types of tree.

- **The female cassowary** mates with several males, laying 6–8 eggs each time. The males care for the young.

- **About 1200 years ago** there were probably 12 million kiwis in New Zealand. Today there are only 70,000.

178

▼ *The nocturnal kiwi's good sense of smell helps it to find worms, insects and spiders in the ground at night.*

Rheas and tinamous

▶ Flocks of rheas live on the pampas grasslands and in open woodland in southeastern South America.

- **The largest bird in South America** is the greater rhea, which stands 1.5 m tall and weighs up to 25 kg.

- **The 45 or so species** of tinamou all live in South America.

> **FASCINATING FACT**
> Male rheas mate with as many as
> 15 females, all of which lay eggs
> in the male's large nest.

- **Most tinamous** can fly, if only for short distances, but they tend to run or hide rather than take to the air.

- **Female tinamous** lay eggs in the nests of more than one male. Males incubate the eggs and feed the chicks.

- **Rheas** feed mostly on plants, but will also eat insects and even lizards when they can.

- **Tinamous** generally eat fruit, seeds and other plant matter, but some species also gobble up insects.

- **Rheas** live in flocks of between 5–50 birds.

- **Rhea feathers** are used to make feather dusters, for sale mainly in the USA and Japan.

- **If threatened**, a rhea lies flat on the ground with its head stretched out in an attempt to hide.

Toucans and honeyguides

- **At 61 cm long**, the toco toucan is the largest toucan. Its colourful beak alone is up to 20 cm long.

- **Although a toucan's beak is large**, it is not heavy. The beak is made of a lightweight material with a honeycomb structure.

- **The black-throated honeyguide** likes to feed on bees and their larvae. When it finds a bees' nest, it leads another creature, such as a honey badger, to the nest and waits while the animal breaks into the nest to feed on the honey. The honeyguide then has its share.

- **There are about 40 species of toucan**. They live in Mexico, Central and South America.

▲ *The black-throated honeyguide is usually a quiet little bird, but it chatters noisily when it wants to attract a helper, such as a honey badger, to a bees' nest, so it can have a share of the honey.*

- **Toucans** feed mostly on fruit, which they pluck from branches with their long beaks. They also eat some insects and small animals such as lizards.

- **Honeyguides** are the only birds that are able to feed on the wax from bees' nests, as well as on the insects themselves.

Beak is about 20 cm long and 7.5 cm deep at the base.

▶ *The toco toucan of Brazil is the largest and best-known of the toucans. It sometimes perches on a branch near another bird's nest to steal the eggs or chicks. Intimidated by the toucan's great beak, the parent bird will not generally attack. When it sleeps, the toucan turns its head to rest its long beak along its back, and folds its tail over its head.*

Strong claws for perching

- **Toucans** usually nest in tree holes. The female lays 2–4 eggs, and the male helps with the incubation, which takes about 15 days.

- **There are about 15 species of honeyguide**. Most live in forests and woodlands in Africa, but there are a few species resident in Asia.

- **Many honeyguides** lay their eggs in the nests of other birds, such as woodpeckers. When they hatch, the young honeyguides kill the young of the host bird.

- **Toucans** are noisy creatures – their loud squawks can be heard nearly 1 km away.

183

Hornbills

- **There are about 45 species of hornbill**, 25 in Africa and 20 in Southeast Asia. Most live among trees.

- **Hornbills** range in size from 38–165 cm. The largest of the family is the great Indian hornbill, and the smallest is the dwarf red-billed hornbill.

- **The eastern yellow-billed hornbill** and the dwarf mongoose have an unusual relationship – they help each other find food and watch out for predators.

- **The female great Indian hornbill** incubates her eggs in a tree hole, the entrance of which is walled up with chewed bark and mud. Through a slit-like opening in the wall, the male passes her food.

- **Hornbills** keep the nest clean by pushing any food waste and droppings out through the slit opening.

- **In parts of South Africa**, the southern ground hornbill is traditionally considered sacred, and is protected.

- **Fruit** is the main food of most hornbills, but the two ground hornbills catch and eat small animals.

◄ *Hornbills are generally fruit-eaters but may also eat small insects, such as locusts, when they are available.*

- **All hornbills** have large beaks. In many species the beak is topped with a casque made of keratin and bone.

- **A male hornbill** may carry more than 60 small fruits at a time to his nest to regurgitate for its young.

- **Hornbills** are the only birds in which two neck vertebrae are fused, possibly to help support the beak's weight.

▲ *The 50-cm long yellow-billed hornbill lives in southern Africa.*

Woodpeckers

- **The woodpecker** feeds by drilling into tree bark with its sharp beak and then inserting its long tongue into the hole to pick out insects living beneath the bark.

- **Woodpeckers** drum on tree trunks with their beaks to signal their ownership of territory or their readiness to mate. The greater spotted woodpecker has been timed making 20 strikes a second.

- **The 200 or so species** of woodpecker live all over the world, except in Antarctica and the far north.

- **The imperial woodpecker**, at 55 cm long, is the biggest of its family. The little scaled piculet, by contrast, is only 8 cm long.

- **Woodpeckers** nest in holes in trees. They may use a hole from a previous year, or dig out a new one for their 2–12 eggs.

▶ *This great spotted woodpecker is sharing a feeder with a siskin. It lives in Europe, parts of Asia and North Africa.*

- **The woodpecker's tongue** is well-adapted for catching insects. It is so long that the woodpecker can stick it out beyond the tip of its beak, and its sticky coating easily mops up its prey.

- **The sapsucker** (woodpecker family) feeds on sweet, sugary sap. It bores a hole in a tree and laps up the sap that oozes out.

- **As well as insects**, the great spotted woodpecker eats the eggs and young of other birds.

- **A woodpecker** may eat up as many as 1000 ants in one feeding session.

- **During autumn**, the acorn woodpecker of North America bores as many as 400 holes in tree trunks and puts an acorn in each one, to store for the winter.

▶ *Woodpeckers have a sharp, chisel-shaped bill for drilling holes through tree trunks. They do this to get at beeswax and insects, such as ants and termites, which are their main sources of food.*

Bee-eaters and relatives

- **The 5 species of tody** are all insect-eating birds that live in the tropical Caribbean islands.

- **Bee-eaters** catch a bee or wasp and kill it by striking it against a branch. The bird rubs the insect against the branch to get rid of the sting.

- **The blue-crowned motmot** has two long tail feathers with racquet-shaped tips. The bird swings its tail like a clock's pendulum as it watches for prey.

- **Motmots** range in size from the 19-cm long tody motmot to the 53-cm long upland motmot.

> ...**FASCINATING FACT**...
> A European bee-eater eats about 200 bees a day. Its summer diet is mainly bumblebees, and in winter it eats honeybees and dragonflies.

- **Motmots** lay their eggs in a chamber at the end of a burrow dug in an earth bank. Both parents incubate the eggs and feed the chicks.

- **The 27 species of bee-eater** are colourful birds that live in southern Europe, Africa, Asia and Australia.

- **The European bee-eater** flies some 16,000 km between Europe, where it breeds, and Africa, where it overwinters.

- **Todies** nest in 30-cm long tunnels, which they dig with their beaks.

- **The 10 species of motmot** live only in forests stretching from Mexico to northern Argentina.

▶ *The white-fronted bee-eater lives in southern Africa.*

Swifts

- **Once a young swift** has left its nest, it may not come to land again until it is about 2 years old and ready to breed. In this time it may fly 500,000 km.

- **The edible-nest swiftlet** makes a nest of its own spit (saliva) and a few feathers on a cave wall. Soup made from these nests is considered a great delicacy in China.

- **Swifts** do almost everything in the air. They eat, drink, court and sometimes even mate on the wing.

- **There are about 70 species of swifts** found all over the world, except in the very far north and far south.

- **The largest swift**, the white-naped swift, is about 25 cm long and weighs 175 g – about the weight of a lemon.

▲ *The common or Eurasian swift is often seen in Europe in the summer, swooping overhead as it hunts for insects. It flies to tropical Africa for the winter.*

- **Trials** with ringed birds have shown that a young common swift that has only just left the nest can fly from London to Madrid in three days.

- **A swift's legs and feet** are so small and weak that it cannot move on the ground. It must land on a cliff ledge or building so it can launch itself into the air again.

- **The cave swiftlet** finds its way in totally dark caves by using a form of echolocation.

- **The African palm swift** glues its nest to the underneath of a palm leaf with its own spit, and glues its eggs to the nest. The parents cling on with their claws while incubating the clutch.

- **When a swift** regurgitates a mouthful of food for its young to eat, it may contain as many as 1000 tiny insects and spiders.

▲ *The nests of certain types of swiftlets are used in Southeast Asia to make soup!*

191

Cuckoos and hoatzin

- **The greater roadrunner**, a type of cuckoo, can move at a speed of 20 km/h or more on land.

- **The Eurasian cuckoo** is a 'brood parasite' – it lays its eggs in the nests of other birds.

- **Most birds** take several minutes to lay an egg, but the cuckoo lays one in just nine seconds, so it can quickly take advantage of any brief absence of the host bird.

- **Of the 129 or so species of cuckoo**, only about 50 lay their eggs in other birds' nests.

- **The 60-cm long hoatzin** (there is only one species) lives deep in South America's rainforest.

- **Hoatzin chicks** leave the nest soon after hatching. Two little claws on each wing help them clamber about.

- **The 22 species of turaco** live only in Africa. Largest is the 90-cm long great blue turaco, weighing 1 kg.

▲ *The hoatzin, from northern South America, has a large plume on its head and, unlike other birds, feeds almost entirely on leaves.*

▲ *These flycatchers are busy feeding a cuckoo chick in their nest.*

- **Turacos** feed mostly on fruit, leaves and flowers, but also catch some insects in the breeding season.

- **Amazingly, the eggs of brood parasite cuckoos** vary in colour and markings according to the host they use. A Eurasian cuckoo's eggs may resemble those of reed warblers, garden warblers or redstarts.

- **The Australian koel** prefers fruit to the caterpillars and other creatures eaten by other cuckoos.

193

Kingfishers

- **The common kingfisher** nests at the end of a 60-cm long tunnel that it excavates in a riverbank. The female lays 4–8 eggs.

- **The tiny African pygmy kingfisher** dives not into water, like the common kingfisher, but into grass, where it snatches grasshoppers and beetles.

- **The 86 or so species of kingfisher** are found all over the world, except parts of the far north.

- **The giant kingfisher** of Africa and the Australian laughing kookaburra are the largest of the family, at about 45 cm long.

- **Common kingfishers** incubate their eggs for 19–21 days, and feed the young for up to 4 weeks.

- **The shovel-billed kingfisher** is armed with its own spade for digging in mud – it uses its large, heavy bill to dig up worms, shellfish and small reptiles.

- **A flash of iridescent** turquoise feathers streaking at high speed along a quiet riverbank indicates the presence of a common or European kingfisher.

◄ *The kingfisher fiercely defends the stretch of riverbank where it feeds and nests.*

- **In the forests of New Guinea**, the male paradise kingfisher shows off its very long tail feathers to females as part of its courtship display.

- **The laughing kookaburra** is named for its call, which sounds like noisy laughter. It makes its call to claim territory. Once one starts, others tend to join in!

- **In northern Australia**, termite mounds are adopted as nest sites by the buff-breasted kingfisher.

▲ *The long, pointed beak of most kingfishers is ideally suited to striking and catching fish.*

195

Nightjars and relatives

- **After hunting for insects** at night, the common potoo rests by day in a tree, where its position and colouration make it look like a broken branch.

- **The 12 species of frogmouth** live in the rainforests of Southeast Asia and Australia.

- **The common poorwill** is one of the few birds known to hibernate. It sleeps in a rock crevice.

- **The bristle-fringed beak** of the nightjar opens very wide to help it snap up moths and beetles at night.

- **The oilbird** is the only bird to feed on fruit at night. Its excellent sense of smell helps it find the oily fruits of palms and laurels in the dark.

- **Oilbird chicks** put on so much weight from their rich diet that they may weigh much more than their parents when they are only a couple of months old.

- **There are about 70 species of nightjars**, found in most warmer parts of the world except New Zealand and southern South America.

- **The oilbird nests** in dark caves, and uses echolocation.

- **An old name for nightjars** is goatsuckers, because people mistakenly thought they saw the birds feeding on goats' milk, when in fact they were snapping up insects disturbed by the animals.

◄ *The potoo lives in forests and woodlands in Mexico and Central and South America.*

◀ *Nightjars are active fliers but rest on the ground during the day where they are well camouflaged.*

...FASCINATING FACT...
So as not to give themselves away by their droppings, potoos squirt out their faeces so that they land well away from their perches.

197

Jacamars and relatives

- **Jacamars** nest in tunnels made in the ground or in termite mounds. They lay 2–4 eggs, which they incubate for 20–23 days.

- **Brightly coloured barbets** live in tropical forests and woodlands in Africa, Asia and South America.

- **At 30 cm long**, the great jacamar is the largest of the 17 species of jacamar. Its beak alone is almost 5 cm long.

- **The white-fronted nunbird** (puffbird family) digs a nesting burrow about 1 m long. The bird lays its eggs in a chamber at the end of the burrow.

- **Biggest of the 75 species of barbet** is the toucan barbet, at 20 cm long. It lives in mountain forests in the northern part of South America.

- **The double-toothed barbet** lays 3–4 eggs, usually in a tree hole. Both parents incubate the eggs and care for the young.

▶ *The crested barbet of southern Africa usually searches for food on the ground.*

- **A jacamar** snaps up an insect in the air, then returns to its perch and bangs the insect against a branch to kill it before eating it.

- **There are about 33 species of puffbird** living in Mexico and Central and South America.

- **Barbet** pairs sing together to keep their relationship close. One bird starts to sing, then stops, and the other bird continues the song within a fraction of a second.

▶ *Jacamars live in Central and South America.*

...FASCINATING FACT...
Puffbirds dart out from a perch
to snatch prey in mid air, or pick
them from leaves.

199

Pigeons and sandgrouse

◄ *Wild rock pigeons live in rocky areas in southern Europe, Asia and northern Africa. The pigeons you see in towns and cities are descended from this species.*

- **The passenger pigeon** was once one of the most common birds in North America – one flock was 480 km long and 1.6 km wide. However, overhunting made the birds rare, and the last passenger pigeon died in captivity in 1914.

- **Both male and female pigeons** can make a milky substance in their crops that they feed to their young.

- **Wood pigeons** feed on leaves, seeds, nuts, berries and some insects, but those living near humans also eat bread and food scraps.

- **At about 70–75 cm long** (nearly as big as a turkey), the Victoria crowned pigeon of New Guinea is the largest member of its family.

- **Pigeon 'races'** are held in which birds return to their homes from 1000 km away.

- **The 16 or so species of sandgrouse** live in southern Europe, Africa and parts of Asia.

- **One adult sandgrouse** was found to have 8000 seeds in its crop.

- **In Christianity**, a dove is often used to symbolize the Holy Spirit. Doves are often released as a gesture of peace and goodwill.

- **There are more than 300 species of pigeon**, and they occur all over the world, except in the far north and Antarctica.

◀ *Sandgrouse usually have grey or brownish feathers with mottled patterns that blend with their desert surroundings.*

...FASCINATING FACT...
A male sandgrouse soaks his belly feathers at a desert waterhole, then flies back to his nest so the chicks can drink from his plumage.

201

Hummingbirds

- **The bee hummingbird** is not much bigger than a bumblebee and, at 6 cm long, is probably the smallest bird.

- **A hummingbird** hovers in front of flowers to collect nectar with its tongue, which has a brushlike tip.

- **When a bee hummingbird hovers**, it beats its wings 200 times a second.

- **The 320 or so species of hummingbird** live in North, Central and South America. Largest is the giant hummingbird, at about 20 cm long and weighing 20 g.

- **At 10.5 cm**, the beak of the sword-billed hummingbird is longer than the rest of its body.

- **Aztec kings** used to wear ceremonial cloaks that were made of hummingbird skins.

- **Tiny ruby-throated hummingbirds** migrate each autumn from the USA across the Gulf of Mexico to Central America. Although only 9 cm long, the bird flies at a speed of about 44 km an hour.

- **The female calliope hummingbird** lays two tiny eggs in a nest made of lichen, moss and spiders' webs. She incubates the eggs for 15 days, and feeds the young for about 20 days until they are able to fly and find food for themselves.

- **Hummingbirds** are the only birds able to fly backwards as well as forwards while they are hovering.

- **A hummingbird** must eat at least half its weight in food each day to fuel its energy needs.

▼ *The male ruby-throated hummingbird courts his mate by flying back and forth in a wide arc like a pendulum, while making a loud humming sound. The female may join in his display.*

Hoopoes and relatives

- **Rollers** have a spectacular courtship flight, rolling and somersaulting as they dive towards land.

- **The eight noisy, insect-eating woodhoopoe** species live in forests in central and southern Africa.

- **A light, coin-shaped mark** on each wing of the broad-billed roller is the reason for its other common name – 'dollar bird'.

- **The cuckoo-roller** lives only in Madagascar and the Comoros Islands, where it catches chameleons and insects.

- **Groups of woodhoopoes** make loud calls and rocking movements, and pass bark to each other, in a display of territorial ownership.

- **The 16 or so species of roller** and ground roller live in southern Europe, Asia, Africa and Australia.

- **The broad-billed roller** catches winged termites in the air. A roller will eat as many as 800 termites a single evening.

◀ *With its decorative crest and striking plumage, the hoopoe is easy to recognize. It lives in Europe, Asia and Africa.*

- **If threatened by birds of prey**, the hoopoe hides by flattening itself on the ground with its wings and tail spread out.

- **The hoopoe** was a symbol of gratitude in ancient Egyptian hieroglyphics. The Egyptians believed that the hoopoe comforted its parents in their old age.

- **The hoopoe** lines its nest with animal excrement, perhaps so that the smell will keep enemies away!

▲ *Rollers use a diving method of hunting that is typical of this group of birds. They catch their prey in mid-air or by swooping to the ground.*

205

Mousebirds and trogons

- **The quetzal** is a species of trogon that lives in Central America. It was sacred to the ancient Maya and Aztec civilizations.

- **The male quetzal's** beautiful tail feathers are up to 1 m long.

- **Mousebirds** get their name from their habit of scurrying around on the ground like mice as they search for seeds and leaves to eat.

- **There are about 37 species of trogon** living in the forests and woodlands of Central America, the Caribbean islands and parts of Africa and Asia.

- **Trogons** range in size from the black-throated trogon, at 23 cm long, to the slightly larger resplendent quetzal, which measures 33 cm in length.

- **The six species of mousebird** are all small, dull-coloured birds of about 10 cm in length. They live in Africa to the south of the Sahara.

◀ Trogons are beautifully coloured tropical birds. They are found in Southeast Asia, the Americas and parts of Africa.

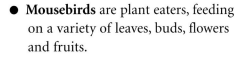

- **Mousebirds** are plant eaters, feeding on a variety of leaves, buds, flowers and fruits.

- **Trogons** nest in tree holes or in old termite mounds or wasps' nests. Both parents incubate the 2–4 eggs for 17–19 days, and both take care of the young.

- **Insects** are the main food of the trogons, but some also eat fruit and catch creatures such as lizards.

▲ *The beautiful quetzal is becoming rare because much of its forest habitat in Central America has been destroyed.*

... FASCINATING FACT ...
The monetary unit of Guatemala is known as the quetzal, after the resplendent quetzal – the country's national bird.

207

Index

A

aboriginal people 105
acorn woodpecker 187
adélie penguins 38
adjutant stork 129
Aepyornis 11
Africa 34, 36, *37*
  babblers 80
  barbets 198, *198*
  bee-eaters 188, *189*
  broadbills 68, *69*
  bulbuls 96
  bustards *136*, 137
  buttonquails 166, *166*
  coursers 152
  cranes *130*, 131
  drongos 90, *91*
  eagles *114*, 116
  finfoots 138
  flamingoes *133*
  flycatchers 58, *58*
  grebes *160*
  guineafowl 170, 171
  herons 134
  honeyguides 183
  hoopoe *204*
  hornbills 184, *185*
  ibises 132
  kingfisher 194
  kites 110
  larks 44, *44*
  mockingbirds 64
  monarch flycatchers 104
  mousebirds 206

nuthatches 62
ostriches *169*
owls *112*
paradise flycatcher 104
pittas 68
quail *170*
rollers 204
sandgrouse 201
shrikes 66
skimmers 147
sparrows 89
starlings 102, *103*
storks 129, *129*
sunbirds 82
swifts *190*
tits 98
trogons 206, *206*
turaco 192
vultures 120, 121
warblers 52
wheatear 78
woodhoopoes 204
wrens 81
African fish eagle 115
African harrier hawk 106
African little sparrowhawk 107
African palm swift 191
African pygmy kingfisher 194
Alaska *95*
albatrosses 27
  laysan 39
  short-tailed 31

wandering 8, 156, *156*, 157
Algeria 63
alpine accentor 64
Alps 62
Amazonian rainforest birds 34
  umbrellabird 55
  wire-tailed manakin *55*
American darter 162
American desert birds 33
American goldfinch 76
American jacana 122
American robin 79
ancient murrelet 154
Andean cock-of-the-rock 55
Andean condor 119, *119*
Andes 140, 177
anhingas **162-163**, *162*
Antarctic,
  migration 28
  penguins 158
  shearwaters 150
  sheathbill 148, *149*
  skuas *148*
  terns 146
  tundra birds 38, 39
antbirds **74-75**, *74*
  ocellated 74
Archaeopteryx 10, *10*
Arctic,
  auks 154, *155*

geese 142
larks 44
migration 28
shearwaters 150
skuas *148*
terns 146
tundra birds 38, 39
wheatear 78
Arctic glaucous gulls 148
Arctic terns 28, 146, 147, *147*
Argentavix 11
Argentina,
  guans 177
  motmot 188
  ovenbirds *86*
argus, crested 173
argus pheasant 172
Aristotle 110
Asia,
  babblers 80
  barbets 198
  bee-eaters 188
  bulbuls 96, 97
  bustard 137, *137*
  buttonquails 166, *166*
  cormorants 162
  coursers 152
  cranes 131
  dipper 79
  drongo 90
  eagles *114*
  fairy-wrens 48
  flamingoes *133*
  flycatchers 58, *58*

grebes 160
grouse 174
honeyguides 183
hoopoe *204*
ibises 132
kites 110
larks 44, *44*
mockingbirds 64
nuthatches 62
oystercatcher *153*
parrots 51
pheasants 172, 173,
    173
red-whiskered
    bulbuls *97*
rollers 204
sandgrouse 201
shrikes 66
sparrows 89
starlings 102
storks 129
sunbirds 82
tits 98
treecreeper *62*
trogon 206
vultures 120
warblers 52
woodpecker *186*
wrens 81
Asian sultan tit 98
Asian watercocks 137
asity 68, 69
Atlantic puffin 154
auklet, least 154
auks 21, **154-155**
    great 11

little 155
Australasia,
    babblers 80
    drongos 91
    fairy-wrens 48
    flycatchers 58
    grebes *160*
    nuthatches 62
    parrots 51
    starlings 102
    warblers 52
Australasian robins 104,
    105
Australasian warblers
    49
Australia 32
    bee-eaters 188
    birds of paradise 100
    blackbirds 79
    bowerbirds 73
    bustards 137
    buttonquails 166
    cassowaries 178
    coursers 152
    cranes 130, 131
    drongo 90, 91
    emu 168
    fairy-wrens 48
    frogmouth 196
    ibises 132
    kingfishers 195
    kites 110
    kookaburra 194
    larks 44
    lyrebirds 84
    megapodes 176

monarch flycatchers
    104
    penguins 158
    pheasants 173
    pittas 68
    plains wanderer 167
    rollers 204
    storks 129
    sunbirds 82
Australian creepers 63
Australian flame robin
    59
Australian koel 193
Australian pelican 14,
    126
Australian songlarks 52
Australian white-
    winged choughs 40
avocets **122-123**
    pied 122, *122*
Azores 76
Aztecs 202, 206

B

babblers **80-81**, *81*
    pale-breasted thrush
    80
bald eagle 114, 115
    endangered species
    31, *31*
    feathers 16
    nests 18, *19*
Baltimore oriole *94*, 95
bar-headed geese 143
barbets 198

crested *198*
    double-toothed 198
    toucan 198
barn owl 26, *26*, 113
barn swallow 42
bataleur eagle *114*, 115
bearded greenbul 96
bearded vulture *120*,
    121
bee hummingbird 9, 18,
    21, 202, *202*
bee-eaters **188-189**
    European 19, 188
    white-fronted *189*
bell-magpies 90, 91
bellbird, three-wattled
    55
berrypecker, crested 82
birds **8-9**
    first **10-11**
    structure of **12-13**
birds of paradise
    100-101
    blue *100*, 101
    king *101*
    ribbon-tailed 100
birds of prey 143, 205
    eagles 116
    falcons *108*, 109
    hawks *107*
    kites 110
    senses *27*
    vultures 118, 119,
        120, 121
bird-watchers 57
bitterns **134-135**, *135*

Index

black-backed gull,
    great 148
    southern 39
black-capped chickadee
    98
black-capped
    donacobious 80
black-collared hawk
    106
black-faced spoonbills
    30
black-headed duck 141
black heron 135
black kite 110
black-naped blue
    monarch 105
black skimmer 146
black swan 142
black-throated
    honeyguide 182,
    182
black-throated trogon
    206
black vultures 119
black-winged stilt 122
blackbirds 79
    New World 94
blackcap 53
blacknecked grebes 161
blue bird of paradise
    100, 101
blue heron, great 134
blue monarch, black-
    naped 105
blue swallow 43
blue tits 98, 99

blue-crowned hanging
    parrots 50
blue-crowned motmot
    188
blue-footed booby 164,
    165
bluebird, fairy 96, 97
bluish flowerpecker 83
boat-billed flycatchers
    57
boatbill,
    yellow-breasted 105
bobolink 94
bohemain waxwing 92,
    92
bokmakierie shrikes 23
Bolivia 160
boobies 164-165
boubou shrikes 25
bowerbirds 72-73, 72
    great grey 73
    regent 73
    satin 72
Brahminy starling 102
Brazil 183
Britain 79
broad-billed roller 204
broadbills 68, 69
brood parasite 192, 193
brown fish owl 112
brown-headed cowbird
    61, 94
brown kiwi 178
brown pelican 126
brown thrasher 65
brown trembler 64

brubru shrike 67
budgerigars 51
buff-breasted flycatcher
    56
buff-breasted kingfisher
    195
bulbuls 96-97
    red-vented 96
    red-whiskered 97
    yellow-vented 96
bullfinch 77
burrowing owl 112
bustards 136-137
    great 136, 137, 137
    kori 136
butcher birds 66
buttonquails 166, 166,
    167
buzzards 110-111
    honey 110
    rough-legged 111

C

cage birds 31, 77, 80
California condors 119
calliope hummingbird
    203
calls 24-25
camouflage,
    bitterns 135
    nightjars 197
    pratincole 152
    tundra birds 38
Canada,
    bobolink 94

migration 28
    tyrant flycatchers 56
canaries 76, 76
cape weaver 46
capercaillie, western
    174
captive breeding 30
    condors 119
    eagles 116
Caribbean 55, 93
    flamingoes 133
    hummingbird 202
    mockingbirds 64
    trogon 206
Carmichael, Hoagy 95
carrion,
    desert birds 33
    parrots 50
    petrels 150
    rainforest birds 34
    tundra birds 39
    vultures 118, 119,
    121
Caspian tern 147
Cassin's hawk eagle 34
cassowaries 34, 178-179
    dwarf 178
catbirds 64, 65, 73
    grey 65
    mockingbirds 65
cattle egrets 36, 135
cave swiftlet 191
cedar waxwing 93
Central Africa 172
Central America 34
    antbirds 74

birds 8
cotingas 55
finfoots 138
flamingoes *133*
hummingbird 202, 203
jacamars *199*
manakins 54
migration 28
ovenbirds 86
parrots 50, 51
potoo *196*
puffbirds 199
quetzal *207*
sunbittern 138
toucans 182
trogon 206
turkeys 174
vermilion flycatcher *57*
vireos 60
wood warblers 94
woodcreeper 87
chachalaca, plain 177
chaffinches 24, *24*
Chatham Island robin 104
Chatham Island tit 104
chestnut sparrow 88
chickadee, black-capped 98
chickens 16, 26
    domestic 172
    prairie 174
chiffchaffs *52*, 53
China,

babblers 80
cranes 130
falcons 109
swifts 190
choughs 40, *41*
    white-winged 40
cinnamon-breasted tody-tyrant 57
cinnamon quail-thrush 32
Clark's nutcracker *63*
cliff swallow 18
cob swans 143
cock-of-the-rocks *54*
    Andean 55
    Guianan 55
cockatoos 51
    palm 50
common guillemot 154, 155
common iora 96, 97
common kestrel 109
common kingfisher 194
common miner 86
common murre 21
common oystercatcher *153*
common pheasants 173
common poorwill 196
common potoo 196
common pratincole 152
common swift 191
common tern 20
common treecreeper *62*
Comoros Islands, roller 204

vangas 66
Compsognathus 10
condors 119, *119*
Congo peafowl 172
coots 136, 137
cormorants **162-163**, *163*
    flightless 162
    great 162
cotingas **54-55**
coursers 152
    cream-coloured 152
cowbird, brown-headed 61, 94
crakes 136
cranes **130-131**, *131*
    crowned 130, *130*
    sandhill 131
    Sarus 130
    Siberian 131
    whooping 130
cream-coloured courser 152
creepers 63, *63*
crested argus 173
crested barbet *198*
crested berrypecker 82
crested grebe, great 160
crested guan 176
crested oropendola 37, 94
crested wood partridge *171*
crimson-breasted shrike 66
crossbill *15*, 76

crows **40-41**, *41*
    hooded *41*
crowned crane 130, *130*
crowned eagle 34
crowned pigeon, Victoria 201
Cuba *202*
cuckoo roller 204
cuckoos 94, 141, **192-193**, *193*
    Eurasian 192, 193
    parental care 23
cuckoo-shrikes 66
curassow 177, *177*
    great 177
    nocturnal 177
curlews 144
    eastern 144
    eskimo 145
    stone 153
    western 144
currawong, pied 90
cygnets 143

D

darters 162
    American 162
Des Murs' wiretail 87
desert birds **32-33**, *32*
    eagles *114*
    larks 44
    sandgrouse *201*
    sparrows 89
    vermilion flycatcher *57*

Index

weavers 46
desert lark 45
dikkop 153
dinosaurs 10
dippers **78-79**, *78*
divers **160-161**
    great northern 160
    white-billed 160
dodo 10
domestic birds,
    canaries 76
    chickens 172
    ducks 141
    guineafowl 171
    turkey 175
donacobious,
    black-capped 80
dotterels 124
double-toothed barbet
    198
doves 201
    mourning 32
drongos 90-91, 90
    fork-tailed 91
    greater racquet-tailed
        90
ducklings 140
ducks **140-141**, *140*
    black-headed 141
    eider 140
    muscovy 34
    parental care 22
    steamer 141
    torrent 140
    wood 141, *141*
dwarf cassowary 178

dwarf red-billed
    hornbill 184

E

eagle owls,
    Eurasian 112
    spectacled 34
eagles **116-117**
    African fish 115
    bald 16, 18, *19*, 31,
        31, 114, 115
    bateleur *114*, 115
    booted 116
    Cassin's hawk 34
    crowned 34
    fish 115
    golden 22, 116, *117*
    harpy **116-117**
    Madagascar fish 115
    martial 116
    nests 18, 19
    parental care 22
    Philippine 116
    rainforest birds *35*
    sea **114-115**
    senses 26
    short-toed 114
    snake **114-115**
    South American
        harpy 116
    Stella's sea *114*
    Verreaux's 116
    white-tailed sea 115
eaglet 116
eastern curlew 144

eastern kingbird 57
eastern phoebe 57
eastern yellow-billed
    hornbill 184
echolocation 191, 196
eclectus parrots 34, *50*
edible-nest swiflet 190
egrets 36
    cattle 135
    great 134, *134*
Egypt,
    hoopoe 205
ibises 132, *133*
    ostrich 168
Egyptian plover 152,
    153
Egyptian vultures 120,
    121
eider duck 140
Eleonora's falcon 109
emperor penguin 39,
    158, *158*, 159, *159*
emu 28, **168-169**
endangered species
    30-31, 130
eskimo curlew 145
Eurasian cuckoo 192,
    193
Eurasian eagle owl 112
Europe,
    bee-eaters 188
    bird of paradise
        feathers 101
    bustard 137, *137*
    buttonquails 166, *166*
    chaffinch *24*

coursers 152
cranes 131
dipper 79
drongo 90
flamingoes *133*
flycatchers 58, *58*
grebes 160
grouse 174
hoopoe *204*
ibises 132
kites 110
larks 44, *44*
mockingbirds 64
nuthatches 62
oystercatcher *153*
partridges 171
pheasants 173, *173*
quail *170*
rollers 204
sandgrouse 201
shrikes 66
sparrows 89
starlings 102
storks 129
swifts 190
tits 98
treecreeper *62*
vultures 120
warblers 52, *53*
woodpecker *186*
wrens 81
European bee-eater 19,
    188
European kingfisher
    194
European nuthatch 63

European robin 79
European snipe 144
European starlings 102, 103

F

fairy bluebird 96, 97
fairy tern 147
fairy-wrens **48-49**
  superb 48, 48
falconets 109
  Philippine 109
falconry 109
falcons **108-109**
  Eleonora's 109
  gyr 108, 108
  peregrine 108, 109, 109
  pygmy 109
Falkland Islands 149
false sunbird, wattled 69
fantails 105
  pied 105
fig bird 91
Fiji petrel 31
finches **76-77**
  chaffinch 24
  snow 88, 88
finfoots 138-139
firewood-gatherer 86
fiscal shrike 66
fish eagles 115
  African 115
  Madagascar 115

fish owl, brown 112
fishing owl, Pel's 112
flame robin, Australian 59
flamingoes 132
  greater 132, 133, 133
flightless birds,
  grebes 160
  kagu 138
  lyrebirds 84
  migration 28
  parrots 50
  penguins 158
  rails 136, 137
  rainforest birds 34
flightless cormorant 162
Floreana mockingbird 31
flowerpeckers 82
  bluish 83
flycatcher 193
  boat-billed 57
  buff-breasted 56
  great-crested 56, 57
  lesser 56
  monarch **104-105**, 104
  narcissus 59
  Old World **58-59**, 59
  paradise 104, 105
  pied 58, 59
  red-breasted 58
  royal 57
  silky 92, 93
  spotted 58, 58, 59

tyrant **56-57**, 56
  vermilion 57, 57
  white-throated jungle 58
fork-tailed drongo 91
fossils 133
fowl,
  mallee 176, 176
  red jungle 172
francolins 171
frigatebirds 156, 157
frogmouth 196
fulmars 150

G

Galapagos Islands,
  cormorants 162
  Floreana mocking bird 31
  penguins 158
gamebirds 174
  quail 170
  rainforest birds 35
gannets **164-165**, 164
  eggs 20
gardener bowerbird, Vogelkop 72
geese **142-143**
  bar-headed 143
  Hawaiian 142
  migration 28, 28
  parental care 22
  red-breasted 143
  snow 28, 142
gentoo penguins 20,

159
gerygones 49
  white-throated 48
giant hummingbird 202
giant kingfisher 194
giant nuthatch 63
giant petrels 150
giant sunbird,
  Sao Tomé 82
gizzard 12
glaucous gulls 148
glossy ibis 133
golden eagle 116, 117
  parental care 22
golden oriole 91
golden plovers 124
golden whistler 49
goldfinches 76, 77, 77
goliath heron 134
goshawks 106, 107
  northern 107
grackles, great-tailed 95
grassland birds **36-37**
great argus pheasant 172
great auk 11
great black-backed gull 148
great blue heron 134
great bustards 136, 137, **137**
great cormorants 162
great crested flycatcher 56, 57
great crested grebe 160, 160, 161

Index

great currasow 177
great egret 134, *134*
great grey bowerbirds 73
great horned owl 37
great Indian hornbill 184
great jacamar 198
great kiskadee 56
great northern diver 160
great skua 39, 148
great-tailed grackles 95
great tits 98, 99
great white pelican 126, *126*
greater flamingo 132, 133, *133*
greater racquet-tailed drongo 90
greater rhea 181
greater roadrunner *33*, 192
greater spotted woodpecker 186, *186*, 187
grebes **160-161**, *161*
  blacknecked *161*
  great crested 160, *160*, 161
  short-winged 160
green-backed heron 135
green broadbill 69
greenbul, bearded 96
grey bowerbird, great 73

grey catbird 65
grey heron 134
grey partridges 171
ground hornbill, southern 36, 184
ground rollers 204
grouse **174-175**
  ruffed 174, 175
  spruce 174, *174*
guans **176-177**
  crested 176, *177*
  white-winged 177
Guatemala 207
Guianan cock-of-the-rock 55
guillemots 154, *154*, *155*
  common 154, 155
guineafowl 170,171
  gulls **148-149**, *149*
  Arctic glaucous 148
  calls 24, 25
  great black-backed 148
  herring 22, 149
  ivory 38, 148
  little 148
  parental care 22
  Ross's 148
  southern black-backed 39
gyr falcon 108, *108*

H

half-footed quails 167
hammerkop 18

hanging parrot, blue-crowned 50
harpy eagles **116-117**
  South American 116
harriers **106-107**
  marsh 106
Hawaiian finches 76, 77
Hawaiian goose *142*, 143
Hawaiian honeycreepers 30
Hawaiian mamo 30
hawfinch 76, 77
hawk eagle, Cassin's 34
hawks **106-107**, *107*
  black-collared 106
  harrier 106
helmet shrikes 66
helmeted guineafowl 171
hemipode quails 167
hens 20
herons **134-135**, *135*
  black 135
  goliath 134
  great blue 134
  green-backed 135
  grey 134
  night 21
herring gulls 22, 149
hibernation 196, *197*
hill mynahs 102
Himalayan monal pheasants 172
Himalayan snowcock 170

Himalayas, accentor 64
  flycatchers 58
  nuthatches 62
hoatzin 34, **192-193**, *192*
honey buzzards 110
honeycreepers, Hawaiian 30
honeyeaters 82, 83
  nests 18
honeyguides **182-183**
  black-throated 182, *182*
hooded crow *41*
hooded pitohui 49
hooded pitta *68*
hoopoes **204-205**
  hornbills 36, **184-185**, *184*
  dwarf red-billed 184
  eastern yellow-billed 184
  great Indian 184
  southern ground 36, 184
  yellow-billed *185*
horned lark *44*, 45
horned owl, great 37
hornero, rufous *86*, 87
house martin *42*
house sparrow 88, 89, *89*
kestrel 109
hummingbirds 14, **202-203**, *203*

bee 9, 21, 202, *202*
calliope 203
giant 202
heartrate 13
nests 18
ruby-throated 16,
203, *203*
sword-billed 202
Hutton's shearwater 31
hyacinth macaw 14, 30,
30

I

ibises **132-133**, *133*
glossy 133
scarlet *132*
Ichthyornis 10, 11
icterids **94-95**
imperial woodpecker
186
India,
cranes 130
flycatchers 58
pheasants *172*
red-whiskered
bulbuls *97*
Indian hornbill, great
184
Indian Ocean 53
Indian pitta 69
intelligence 40, *41*
iora, common 96, 97
ivory gulls 38, 148

J

jacamars **198-199**, *199*
great 198
jacanas 123, *123*
American 122
pheasant-tailed 122,
123
jackdaws 40, 41
Japan,
cranes 130
crow family 40
herons 135
rheas 181
jays 40
jungle flycatcher,
white-throated 58
jungle fowl, red 172

K

Kabylie nuthatch 63
kagu 138, 139
kakapo 50
kea 50
Kentish plover 124
kestrel, common 109
killdeer 124
king bird of paradise
101
king of Saxony bird of
paradise 100
king penguins 158
king vultures 34, 118,
119

kingbird, eastern 57
kingfishers **194-195**,
194
African pygmy 194
buff-breasted 195
common 194
European 194
giant 194
paradise 195
shovel-billed 194
kiskadee, great 56
kites **110-111**, *111*
black 110
red 111
snail 110
kittiwake 149, *149*
kiwis 12, 77, **178-179**,
179
brown 178
senses 27
koel, Australian 193
kokako 90
kookaburra, laughing
194, 195
kori bustard *136*

L

lappet-faced vultures
121
lapwings **124-125**
larks **44-45**
desert 45
horned *44*, 45
shore 44, *44*, 45
thick-billed 45

laughing kookaburra
194, 195
laysan albatross 39
leafbirds 97
least auklet 154
least sandpiper 144
leiothrix, red-billed 80
lesser flycatcher *56*
lily-trotter *123*
limpkin 130
little auk 155
little gull 148
little scaled piculet 186
little sparrowhawk,
African 107
loggerhead shrike 67
long-billed
woodcreeper 87
long-tailed tits 98, 99
longclaws 44
yellow-throated 44
lories 51
lyrebirds **84-85**, *85*
superb 84

M

macaws 50, 51
hyacinth 14, 30, *30*
endangered species
30, *30*
rainforest birds *35*
red-and-green 51
scarlet 50, *51*
Madagascar,
Aepyornis 11

Index

asity 68
fish eagle 115
roller 204
vangas 66
magnificent riflebird 100
magpies 40
malimbe, red-vented 47
mallee fowl 176, *176*
mamo, Hawaiian 30
man o' war *157*
manakins **54-55**
little wire-tailed *55*
wire-tailed 55
mandarins *140*
manx shearwater 151, *151*
marabou stork 129
marsh harrier 106
marsh warbler 53
martial eagle 116
martins **42-43**, *42*
house *42*
purple 42
sand 42, 43
white-eyed river 42
meadow pipit 45
meadowlark, western 37
Mediterranean gannet *164*
megapodes **176-177**
merganser 141
red-breasted 141
mesites **166-167**
Mexico,
antbirds 74

cotingas 55
desert birds 32
motmot 188
ovenbirds 86
potoo *196*
puffbirds 199
toucans 182
turkeys 174
woodcreeper 87
migration **28-29**, *28*
bobolink 94
hummingbird 203
martins 42, 43
nuthatches *62*
poorwill *197*
quail *170*
skuas *148*
terns 146
tundra birds 39
mimicry,
mockingbirds 64, *64*, 65, *65*
starlings 102
warblers 53
miner,
campo 87
common 86
mistletoe bird 83
mockingbirds **64-65**, *65*
Floreana 31
monal pheasant,
Himalayan 172
monarch, black-naped blue 105
monarch flycatchers **104-105**, *104*

moorhens 136, 137
moruk 178
motmots 188
blue-crowned 188
tody 188
turquoise-browed 19
upland 188
moulting 16
Mount Everest 143
mourning dove 32
mousebirds **206-207**
murre, common 21
murrelet, ancient 154
muscovy duck 34
mute swans 142
mynahs, hill 102

N

narcissus flycatcher *59*
Native Americans 113
nectar,
bulbuls 97
drongos 91
finches 77
hummingbirds 14, 202, *203*
starlings 102
sunbird 69, 82
New Caledonia 40
New Guinea,
birds of paradise 100, 101
bowerbirds 73
fairy-wrens 48
kingfishers 195

pigeons 201
rainforest birds 34
New World blackbirds 94
New World vultures **118-119**
New York, USA 89
falcons 109
starlings 103
New Zealand,
blackbirds 79
drongos 91
endangered species 31
kiwis 178
moa 11
parrots 50
plovers 124, *125*
rails 136
sunbirds 82
takahe 137
wattlebirds 90
wrens 84
night heron 21
nightingale 79
nightjars **196-197**, *197*
beak 14
desert birds 33
nests 18
niltava, rufous-bellied 58
nocturnal curassow 177
North Africa *44*
North America,
babblers 80
cranes 131

dipper 79
ducks *141*
grassland birds 37
grouse 174
hummingbird 202
ibises 132
larks 44, *44*
migration 28
mockingbirds 64
nuthatches 62
partridges 171
pheasants 173, *173*
pigeons 200
shrikes 66
skimmers 147
starlings 102
storks 129
thrushes 79
tits 98
tyrant flycatchers *56*
vireos 60, *60*
vultures 118
warblers 52
wood warblers 94
woodpecker *186*, 187
wrens 81
North Atlantic gannet *164*
North Pacific 39
auks 154, *155*
northern diver, great 160
northern goshawk 107
northern hemisphere 43
northern mockingbird *64*, 65

northern shrike 66
northern wrens 81
nostrils 12, *13*
    drongos *91*
    kiwis 178
    shearwaters 150
nunbird, white-fronted 198
nutcrackers 40
    Clark's 63
nuthatches **62-63**, *62*
    European 63
    giant 63
    Kabylie 63
    red-breasted 62, *62*

O

oilbird 196
Old World flycatchers **58-59**, *59*
Old World oriole 90
Old World sparrows **88-89**
Old World vultures 118, **120-121**
olive oropendola 95
openbill stork 129
orders of birds 8
oriole,
    Baltimore *94*, 95
    golden 91
    Old World 90
ornithologists 57
oropendola,
    crested 37, 94

olive 95
osprey 8, *9*, **110-111**, *110*
ostriches 9, **168-169**, *169*
    ancestor 11
    eggs 20
    senses 26
    toes 14
ovenbirds **86-87**
owls **112-113**, *113*
    barn 26, *26*, 113
    brown fish 112
    burrowing 112
    desert birds 33
    eggs 21
    Eurasian eagle 112
    grassland birds 37
    great horned 37
    least pygmy 112
    parrots 50
    snowy 38, *38*, *113*
    spectacled eagle 34
oxpecker 37
    yellow-billed 36
oystercatchers **152-153**
    common *153*

P

Pacific islands,
    buttonquails 166
    crow family 40
    kagu 138
    megapodes 176
    monarch flycatchers

104
tundra birds 39
Pakistan *172*
pale-breasted thrush babbler 80
palm cockatoo 50
palm swift, African 191
palm-nut vultures 120
palmchats 92, 93
paradise flycatcher 104, *105*
paradise kingfisher 195
paradise whydah 47
parental care **22-23**
    barbets 198
    bulbuls 96
    motmot 188
    phalaropes 145
    pratincole 152
    skuas 148
    sunbittern 139
    trogons 207
    vultures 121
parrots **50-51**, *51*
    blue-crowned hanging 50
    calls 24
    eclectus 34, *50*
    endangered species 30
    owl 50
    rainforest birds 34, *35*
    toes 14
parson bird 82
partridges **170-171**

Index

crested wood *171*
grey 171
red-legged 171
passenger pigeon 200
passerines *15*, 59
peacocks 172, *172*, 173
feathers *16*
peafowl 172
Pel's fishing owl *112*
pelicans **126-127**, *127*
Australian 14, 126
brown 126
great white 126, *126*
parental care 22
white 126
penduline tit 98
penguins **158-159**
adelie 38
colonies 148
eggs 20
emperor 39, 158, *158*, 159, *159*
gentoo 20, 159
king 158
migration 28
pen swans 143
perching birds 8, 14, *15*
peregrine falcon 108, 109, *109*
Peru,
flycatchers 57
grebes 160
pesticides 31
pet trade *30*
petrels **150-151**, *151*
Fiji 31

giant 150
storm 39, *150*
phalaropes 144, 145
pheasant-tailed jacanas 122, 123
pheasants **172-173**
common 173
great argus 172
ring-necked *173*
Philippine creepers 63
Philippine eagle 116
Philippine falconet 109
Philippine flycatchers 58
phoebe, eastern 57
piculet, little scaled 186
pied avocets 122, *122*
pied currawong 90
pied fantail 105
pied flycatchers 58, 59
pied wagtail 45
pigeons **200-201**, *200*
passenger 200
Victoria crowned 201
wood 200
pipits 44
meadow 45
pitohui, hooded 49
pittas **68-69**
hooded *68*
rainbow 69
red-bellied *68*
plain chachalaca 177
plains wanderer 167
plantcutters 60
play 107

plovers **124-125**
Egyptian 152, 153
golden 124
Kentish 124
ringed *153*
spur-winged 124
plumage,
antbirds 74, *74*
bitterns *135*
ducks *140*
fairy-wrens *48*
finches *76*
flycatchers 57, *59*
gamebirds *174*
herons 134
hoopoe *204*
ibises *132*
kittiwake *149*
oriole *94*
owls *113*
parrots *50*
pheasants *173*
plover *153*
rainforest birds 34
sandgrouse 201
sparrows 89
starlings *102*
sunbirds 82
sunbittern *139*
plumes,
birds of paradise 100
hoatzin *192*
poisonous birds 49
poisonous plants 50
polar birds **38-39**
polar skua, south 149

pollen,
starlings 102
sunbirds 82
poorwills 33, *197*
common 196
potoo *196*, 197
prairie chickens 175
prairies 37
pratincole 152
common 152
preening 16
prions 150, 151
ptarmigan, willow 38, *39*
puffback 66
puffbirds 198, 199
puffins 154, 155
Atlantic 154
tufted 39, *155*
purple martins 42
pygmy falcons 109
pygmy owl, least 112
pygmy seed-snipe 153
pygmy tyrant, short-tailed 57

Q

quail-thrush, cinnamon 32
quails 37, 166, 170, *170*
half-footed 167
hemipode 167
quelea, red-billed 8, 36, *37*, 46
quetzal 206, 207, *207*

R

races, pigeon 201
racquet-tailed drongo,
    greater 90
rails **136-137**
    Inaccessible Island
        136
rainbow pittas 69
rainforest birds **34-35**,
    35
    bulbuls 96
    fairy-wrens 48
    frogmouth 196
    hoatzin 192
    ovenbirds 86
    parrots 50, *51*
    pheasants 172
    pittas *68*
    trumpeters 130
    vultures 118
    wire-tailed manakin
        55
ravens 40, *41*
razorbills 154
red-and-green macaw
    51
red-bellied pitta *68*
red-billed hornbill,
    dwarf 184
red-billed leiothrix 80
red-billed quelea 8, 36,
    37, 46
red-billed scythebill 86
red bishop 47

red-breasted flycatchers
    58
red-breasted geese 143
red-breasted merganser
    141
red-breasted nuthatch
    62, *62*
red-eyed vireo 60, *60*
red-footed booby *165*
red jungle fowl 172
red kite 111
red-legged partridge
    171
red-legged seriema 36
red siskins 31
red-vented bulbuls 96
red-vented malimbe 47
red-whiskered bulbuls
    97
redstarts 193
reed warblers 193
    great *53*
regent bowerbirds 73
reptiles 10, 12
resplendent quetzal *35*
rheas 36, **180-181**, *180*
    greater 181
ribbon-tailed bird of
    paradise 100
riflebird, magnificent
    100
rifleman 84
ring-necked pheasant
    173
ringed birds 191
ringed plover *153*

river martin, white-
    eyed 42
roadrunner, greater *33*,
    192
robins 79
    American 79
    Australasian 104, 105
    Australian flame 59
    Chatham Island 104
    European *79*
    rose 105
rock warbler 48
rockfowl 81
    white-necked 80
rollers 204, *205*
    broad-billed 204
    cuckoo 204
    ground 204
Rome 43, 173
rooks 40, *41*
rose-coloured starling
    103
rose robin 105
Ross's gull 148
Ross, James Clark 148
rough-legged buzzard
    111
royal flycatcher 57
ruby-throated
    hummingbird 16,
    203, *203*
ruffed grouse 174, 175
rufous-bellied niltava
    58
rufous-breasted castle
    builder 19

rufous hornero *86*, 87
rufous scrub-bird 84

S

saddlebill 129
Sahara Desert 28
saliva 190
sand martin 42, 43
sandgrouse 32, **200-
    201**, *201*
sandhill crane 131
sandpipers **144-145**,
    144
    least 144
Sao Tomé giant sunbird
    82
sapsucker 187
Sardinia 109
Sarus crane 130
satin bowerbirds 72
scaled piculet, little 186
scarlet ibises *132*
scarlet macaw 50, *51*
scrub-bird 84
    rufous 84
scrubwrens 49
scythebill, red-billed 86
sea eagles **114-115**
    Stella's *114*
    white-tailed 115
seabirds 10, *11*, **156-157**
secretary bird 36, *36*
sedge warbler 24
seed-snipe, pygmy 153
sense of smell 12, 27

Index

kiwi *179*
migration 28
oilbird 196
pittas 69
shearwaters 150, *150*
vultures 118
senses 15, **26-27**
seriema 139
red-legged 36
sharpbill 60
shearwaters 23, **150-151**
Hutton's 31
manx 151, *151*
sheathbill *149*
snowy 148
shell 21
shoebill 128
shore lark 44, *44*, 45
short-tailed albatross 31
short-tailed pygmy tyrant 57
short-toed eagles 114
short-winged grebe 160
shovel-billed kingfisher 194
shrikes **66-67**, *67*
bokmakierie *23*
boubou 25
brubru 67
crimson-breasted *66*
fiscal 66
helmet 66
loggerhead 67
northern 66
Siberian cranes 131

Siberian warblers 52
sicklebilled vanga *66*, 67
sight 26, 27
silky flycatcher 92, 93
siskin 77, *186*
red 31
skeleton 13, 16
skimmers **146-147**, *146*
black 146
skin,
bird of paradise 101
hummingbird 202
thickheads 49
vultures 118
skuas 148, *148*
great 39, 148
south polar 149
skull 164
skylarks *25*, 45
smell, sense of 27
birds 12
kiwi *179*
migration 28
oilbird 196
pittas 69
shearwaters 150, *150*
vultures 118
snail kite 110
snake bird 162
snake eagles **114-115**
snipe 144
European 144
snow finch 88, *88*
snow geese 28, 142
snowcock, Himalayan 170

snowy owls 38, *38*, 113
snowy sheathbill 148
sociable weaver 46
songbirds 25
crow family 40
dipper 78
flycatchers *59*
lyrebirds 84
pittas 69
songlarks, Australian 52
songs **24-25**
bablers 80
barbets 199
blackbirds 79
lyrebirds 84
mockingbirds 65
skylark 45
thrushes *12*, 79
vireos 61
warblers 52, *52*, 53
South Africa,
hornbills 184
oystercatcher *153*
penguins 158
South African grassbird 52
South American birds 8
antbirds 74
barbet 198
bobolink 94
cotingas 55
dipper 79
ducks 140
finfoots 138
grassland birds 36, 37

harpy eagle 116
hoatzin 192, *192*
hummingbird 202
ibises 132
jacamars *199*
larks 44
manakins 54
migration 28
mockingbirds 64
ovenbirds 86
parrots 50, 51
plantcutters 60
potoo *196*
puffbirds 199
rainforest birds 34
rheas *180*, 181
seed-snipe 153
sheathbill *149*
skimmers 147
storks 129
sunbittern 138
tapaculos 74
tinamou 181
toucans 182
tyrant flycatchers 56, *56*
vermilion flycatcher 57, *57*
vireos 60
vultures 118
warblers 52wood
warblers 94
woodcreeper 87
yellow warbler *95*
South Atlantic Ocean 136

south polar skua 149
Southeast Asia,
    broadbill 68
    cranes 130
    drongos 91
    fairy-wrens 48
    finfoots 138
    flycatchers 58
    frogmouth 196
    hornbills 184
    monarch flycatchers
        104
    partridges *171*
    pheasants 172
    pittas 68
    skimmers 147
    sunbirds 82
    swiftlets *191*
    trogons *206*
southern black-backed
    gull 39
southern ground
    hornbill 36, 184
Southwest Asia,
    herons 134
    ostriches 168
    sparrows 88
sparrowhawk 106, *106*
    little 107
sparrows,
    chestnut 88
    desert 89
    house 88, 89, *89*
    Old World **88-89**
spectacled eagle owl 34
spiders' web nests 18

broadbill 69
fairy-wrens 48
flycatchers 58
hummingbird 203
monarchs 105, *105*
vireos 61
warblers 53
splendid starling *103*
spoonbills 132
    black-faced 30
spotted flycatchers 58,
    58, 59
spotted woodpecker,
    greater 186, *186*,
    187
spruce grouse 174, *174*
spur-winged plovers
    124
Sri Lanka *172*
starlings **102-103**, *102*
    Brahminy 102
    European 102, 103
    rose-coloured *103*
    senses 26
    splendid 103
    wattled 102
steamer ducks 141
Stella's sea eagles *114*
Stephen Island wren 84
stilts 122
    black-winged 122
stone curlew 153
storks **128-129**, *128*
    adjutant 129
    marabou 129
    openbill 129

white 129
white-billed 128
wood 129
storm petrel 39, *150*
sultan tit 98
sunbirds **82-83**, *82*
    Sao Tomé giant 82
    wattled false 69
sunbittern 34, 138, *139*
sungrebe 138, 139
superb fairy-wren 48,
    48
superb lyrebirds 84
superstitions 40
swallows **42-43**, *43*
    barn 42
    blue 43
    cliff 18
    migration 28
    wood 91
swans 142-143, 143
    black 142
    mute 142
    parental care 22, *22*
    trumpeter 142
    tundra 142
    whistling 16
    whooper 142
swiftlets *191*
    cave 191
    edible-nest 190
swifts 14, **190-191**, *190*,
    203
    African palm 191
    common 191
    white-naped 190

sword-billed humming
    bird 202
syrinx 24

T

tail feathers 144
    bird of paradise 100,
        101, *101*
    bluish flowerpecker
        83
    drongos 90
    ibises *132*
    kingfishers 195
    kittiwake *149*
    monarchs 104
    motmots 188
    nuthatches 62
    pheasants 173
    storks 129
    tits 99
    trogon 206
    whydah 47
    wire-tailed manakin
        55
    wiretail 87
tailorbird 53
takahe 137
tapaculos **74-75**
tastebuds 26
teeth 10, 12, *13*, 75
terns 23, **146-147**
    Arctic 28, 146
    Caspian 147
    common 20
    fairy 147

Index

territory,
  bishop 47
  flycatchers 57
  hoopoes 204
  kingfishers 195
  woodpecker 186
Thailand 42
thick-billed lark 45
thick-knees 153
thickheads 48, 49
thornbills 49
thrashers 64
  brown 65
three-wattled bellbird
  55
throat pouch 126
thrush babbler, pale-
  breasted 80
thrushes *12*, **78-79**
tinamous **180-181**
tits **98-99**
  blue 98, *99*
  Chatham Island 104
  great *98*, 99
  long-tailed 98, 99
  penduline 98
  sultan 98
  willow 99
toco toucan 182, *183*
tody 188
tody motmot 188
tody-tyrant, cinnamon-
  breasted 57
Tonga 176
tongue,
  flamingo 132

hummingbirds *14*,
  202
penguins 159
starlings 102
sunbirds 82
woodpecker 186, 187
tool-use 40
torrent ducks 140
toucan barbet 198
toucans 21, *35*, **182-183**
  toco 182, *183*
treecreepers 62, 63
  common 62
tremblers 64
  brown 64
trogons **206-207**, *206*
  black-throated 206
tropicbirds 157
  white-tailed 156
trumpeter swans 142
trumpeters **130-131**
tufted puffin 39, *155*
tundra birds **38-39**,
  111, 142
turacos 192, 193
turkeys **174-175**, *175*
  domestic 174
turquoise-browed
  motmot 19
tyrant flycatchers
  56-57, *56*
tyrant, short-tailed
  pygmy 57

U

ultra-violet light 109
umbrellabird,
  Amazonian 55
USA,
  bobolink 94
  desert birds 32, *33*
  eagles 115
  guans 177
  hummingbird 203
  orioles 95
  rheas 181
  sparrows 89, *89*
  starlings 103
  turkeys 174
  tyrant flycatchers 56
  vermilion flycatcher
    57

V

vangas **66-67**
  sickle-billed 66, *67*
vermilion flycatcher 57,
  57
vertebrae 185
Victoria crowned
  pigeon 201
vireos **60-61**, *61*
  black-capped 60
  red-eyed 60, *60*
Vogelkop gardener 72
vultures 11
  bearded *120*, 121

black 119
Egyptian 120, *121*
king 34, 118, 119
lappet-faced 121
New World **118-119**,
  118
Old World 118,
  120-121
palm-nut 120
turkey *33*, 118
white-backed 121
vulturine guineafowl
  170

W

wading birds,
  avocets 122
  sandpipers *144*
  storks 128
wagtails **44-45**
  pied *45*
  willie 105
wallcreeper 62
wanderer, plains 167
wandering albatross 8,
  156, *156*, 157
warblers **52-53**
  Aldabra 53
  Australasian 49
  garden 193
  grasshopper 52
  great reed *53*
  Kirtland's 94
  marsh 53
  reed 193

rock 48
sedge 24
willow 52, *52*, 53
wood **94-95**
yellow 95, *95*
warm-blooded animals 12
waterbirds 14
watercocks, Asian 137
wattlebirds 90
wattled false sunbird 69
wattled starling 102
wattles,
  guans *177*
  pheasants *173*
  vultures 118
waxbills 46
waxwings **92-93**, *93*
  bohemian 92, *92*
  cedar 93
weavers 46-47
  baya 47
  cape *46*
  sociable 46
webbed feet 14
weight 12
weka 136
West Africa *69*
western capercaillie 174
western curlew 144
western meadowlark 37
whale-billed stork 128
wheatear 78
whistler, golden 49
whistling swan 16
white pelican 126

great 126, *126*
white-backed vulture 121
white-billed diver 160
white-breasted mesites *167*
white-eyed river martin 42
white-fronted bee-eater *189*
white-fronted nunbird 198
white-naped swift 190
white-necked rockfowl 80
white stork 129
white-tailed sea eagle 115
white-tailed tropicbird 156
white-throated gerygone 48
white-throated jungle flycatcher 58
white-winged choughs 40
white-winged guan 177
whooper swans 142
whooping crane 130
whydahs 46
  paradise 47
wild turkeys 174, *175*
willie wagtail 105
willow ptarmigan 38, *39*
willow tit 99

willow warbler 52, *52*, 53
wing claps 25
wings 13
  albatross 156, *157*
  antbirds 75
  auks 155
  cormorants 162
  ducks 141
  eagles *117*
  falcons 109
  grouse 174
  herons 135
  hummingbird 202, *203*
  mesites 166
  pelicans 126
  penguins 158
  pheasants 172
  sunbittern 138, *139*
  sungrebe 138
  waxwings 92, *93*
wingspan,
  booby 165
  bustard *137*
  cranes *131*
  eagles 116
  flamingoes 133
  osprey *110*
  vultures 119, 121
wire-tailed manakin 55
  little *55*
wood duck 141, *141*
wood partridge, crested *171*
wood pigeons 200

wood stork 129
wood swallows 91
wood warblers **94-95**
woodcreepers 19, 86, 87
  long-billed 87
woodhoopoes 204
woodpeckers 183, **186-187**
woodpigeons 25
wrens **80-81**, *81*
  cactus 80, *80*
  New Zealand 84
  northern 81
  Stephen Island 84
  winter 81
wren-tit 80
wrist bones 13
wrybill 124, *125*

Y

yellow-billed hornbill *185*
  eastern 184
yellow-billed oxpecker 36
yellow-breasted boatbill 105
yellow-throated longclaw 44
yellow-vented, bulbuls 96
young birds 8, 9

Acknowledgements

The publishers would like to thank the following artists who have contributed to this book:

L R Galante (Galante Studio), Roger Goringe,
Alan Harris, Mike Hughes, Roger Kent (Illustration),
Mick Loates (Linden Artists), Kevin Maddison,
Steve Roberts, Eric Robson, Rudi Vizi

The publishers would like to thank the following sources for
the use of their photographs:

All other pictures from the Miles Kelly Archives,
Corel Corporation; Digital Stock Corp;
Digital Vision; PhotoDisk